MESA and Trading Market Cycles

WILEY TRADER'S ADVANTAGE SERIES

John F. Ehlers, *MESA and Trading Market Cycles*
Robert Pardo, *Design, Testing, and Optimization of Systems*

MESA and Trading
Market Cycles

John F. Ehlers

Series Editor: Perry J. Kaufman

John Wiley & Sons, Inc.
New York • Chichester • Brisbane • Toronto • Singapore

Copyright © 1992 by John F. Ehlers
Published by John Wiley & Sons, Inc.

Library of Congress Cataloging-in-Publication Data

Ehlers, John F., 1933–
    MESA and trading market cycles / by John F. Ehlers.
       p.   cm. — (Wiley trader's library : 1949)
    Includes index.
    ISBN 0-471-54943-6 (cloth)
    1. MESA (Computer program) 2. Futures—Computer programs.
  3. Options (Finance)—Computer programs. 4. Business cycles—
Computer programs. I. Title. II. Series.
HG6024.A3E43 1992
332.63'2'0285—dc20   91-40274

Printed in the United States of America

10 9 8 7 6 5 4 3 2 1

Printed and bound by Courier Companies, Inc.

To Elizabeth

ACKNOWLEDGMENTS

My thanks to Dr. Alexander Elder for encouraging me to focus my engineering talent and research in the area of cycles in the market and to Perry Kaufman for helping me present the results in a format useful to traders.

THE TRADER'S ADVANTAGE SERIES PREFACE

The Trader's Advantage series is a new concept in publishing for traders and analysts of futures, options, equity and generally all world economic markets. Books in the series present single ideas with only that background information needed to understand the content. No long introductions, no definitions of the futures contract, clearing house and order entry. Focused.

The Futures and Options Industry is no longer in its infancy. From its role as an agricultural vehicle it has become the alterego of the most active world markets. The use of EFP's (Exchange for Physicals) in currency markets makes the selection of physical or futures markets transparent, in the same way the futures markets evolved into the official pricing vehicle for world grain. With a single telephone call a trader or investment manager can hedge a stock portfolio, set a crossrate, perform a swap, or buy the protection of an inflation index. The classic regimes can no longer be clearly separated.

And this is just the beginning. Automated exchanges are penetrating traditional open outcry markets. Even now, from the time the transaction is completed in the pit, everything else is electronic. "Program trading" is the automated response to the analysis of a computerized ticker tape, and just the tip of the inevitable evolutionary process. Soon the executions will be computerized and then we won't be able to call anyone to complain about a fill. Perhaps we won't even have to place an order to get a fill.

Market literature has also evolved. Many of the books written on trading are introductory. Even those intended for more advanced audiences often include a review of contract specifications and market mechanics. There are very few books specifically targeted for the experienced and professional traders and analysts. *The Trader's Advantage* series changes all that.

This series presents contributions by established professionals and exceptional research analysts. The authors' highly specialized talents have been applied primarily to futures, cash and equity markets, (but are often general in applicable to price forecasting) across all markets. Topics in the series will include trading systems and individual techniques, all are a necessary part of the development process which is intrinsic to improving price forecasting and trading.

These works are creative, often state-of-the-art. They offer new techniques, in-depth analysis of current trading methods, or innovative and enlightening ways of looking at still unsolved problems. The ideas are explained in a clear, straightforward manner with frequent examples and illustrations. Because they do not contain unnecessary background material they are short and to the point. They require careful reading, study and consideration. In exchange, they contribute knowledge to help build an unparalleled understanding of all areas of market analysis and forecasting.

MESA

John Ehlers is the consummate technical analyst. Eminently qualified, highly experienced and deeply committed, he is willing to share the method behind his efforts. MESA (Maximum Entropy Spectral Analysis) is primarily the identification of short-term cycles for trading. But it is taken much further.

Cycles alone are an interesting application of price analysis because they forecast, rather than explain, price movement. The goal of explaining price action is to be able to say what prices are doing now, in context of the interval of observation. Forecasting attempts to predict what prices will do at some future time. Explaining always includes a lag, while forecasting does not.

Ehlers does even more. MESA forecasts only short-term cycles. Trading based on this faster movement can reduce risk and be more responsive to changing situations.

The complete method also provides a surprisingly practical approach to trading by specifying when trading signals should follow the short-term cycles and when a trend is the dominant factor. It is a very intriguing way of distinguishing sideways from trending markets—and of profiting from them.

Ehlers' presentation is rigorous and parts of the description will require a modest but working knowledge of mathematics or statistics. But it is not necessary to solve the formulas in order to benefit from the method. Once the principle is understood, the solution may be found using statistical software packages or MESA itself, both commercially available.

Perry J. Kaufman

Bermuda
May 1992

FOREWORD

Modern computers, available to every trader, have dramatically altered the way technical analysts study the market. The studies are not only more complex and detailed but also broader. The studies are broader because greater understanding of underlying principles and insight have resulted from the overview enabled by the greater computational power.

Cycle analysis is one of the elements that have been profoundly affected by computers because these studies are computationally intensive. The very accomplishment of the calculations has led to a greater appreciation that the market is dynamic rather than static. Through the use of cycle analysis, traders can now model the market and use the model to adapt strategies to the current market conditions.

This book establishes a philosophical basis for the existence of cycles in the market and describes the basic characteristics of cycles. Traditional moving averages, momentum functions, and indicators are described again from the cyclic perspective to establish effects in the dynamic market. All the principles are brought together in trading examples to show how trading strategy can be altered to improve the probability of establishing successful trades.

John F. Ehlers

Goleta, California
April 1992

CONTENTS

1

WHY CYCLES EXIST
IN THE MARKET

Technical analysis of the market is successful because the market is not always efficient. Discernible events that occur in chart patterns, such as double tops and Elliott waves, enable trading to be guided by technical analysis. Cycles are one of these discernible events that occur and are identifiable by direct measurement. Identification of cycles does not take a lifetime of experience or an expert system. Cycles can be measured directly, either by a simple system such as measuring the distance between successive lows or by a sophisticated computer software program such as MESA.

The fact that cycles exist does not imply that they exist all the time. Cycles come and go. External events sometimes dominate and obscure existing cycles. Experience shows that cycles useful for trading are present only about 15 to 30 percent of the time. This corresponds remarkably with J. M. Hurst's statement that "23% of all price motion is oscillatory in nature and semi-predictable."[1] It is analogous to the problems of the trend-follower, who finds that the markets "trend" only a small percentage of the time.

HISTORICAL PERSPECTIVE

Cyclic recurring processes observed in natural phenomena by humans since the earliest times have embedded the basic concepts used in modern spectral estimation. Ancient civilizations were able to design calendars and time measures from their observations of the periodicities in the length of day, the length of the year, the seasonal changes, the phases of the moon, and the motion of the planets and stars. Pythagoras developed a relationship between the periodicity of musical notes produced by a fixed tension string and a number representing the length of the string in the sixth century B.C. He believed that the essence of harmony was inherent in the numbers. Pythagoras extended the relationship to describe the harmonic motion of heavenly bodies, describing the motion as the "music of the spheres."

Sir Isaac Newton provided the mathematical basis for modern spectral analysis. In the seventeenth century, he discovered that sunlight passing through a glass prism expanded into a band of many colors. He determined that each color represented a particular wavelength of light and that the white light of the sun contained all wavelengths. He invented the word *spectrum* as a scientific term to describe the band of light colors.

Daniel Bournoulli developed the solution to the wave equation for the vibrating musical string in 1738. Later, in 1822, the French Engineer Jean Baptiste Joseph Fourier extended the wave equation results by asserting that any function could be represented as an infinite summation of sine and cosine terms. The mathematics of such representation has become known as harmonic analysis due to the harmonic relationship between the sine and cosine terms. *Fourier transforms,* the frequency description of time domain events (and vice versa) have been named in his honor.

Norbert Wiener provided the major turning point for the theory of spectral analysis in 1930, when he published his classic paper "Generalized Harmonic Analysis." Among his contributions were precise statistical definitions of *autocorrelation* and *power spectral density* for stationary random processes. The use of Fourier transforms, rather than the *Fourier series* of traditional harmonic analysis, enabled Wiener to define spectra in terms of a continuum of frequencies rather than as discrete harmonic frequencies.

John Tukey is the pioneer of modern empirical spectral analysis. In 1949 he provided the foundation for spectral estimation using correlation estimates produced from finite time sequences. Many of the terms of modern spectral estimation (such as aliasing, windowing, prewhitening, tapering, smoothing, and decimation) are attributed to Tukey. In 1965 he collaborated with Jim Cooley to describe an efficient algorithm for digital computation of the Fourier transform. This *fast Fourier transform* (FFT) unfortunately is not suitable for analysis of market data, as we will develop in later chapters.

The work of John Burg was the prime impetus for the current interest in high-resolution spectral estimation from limited time sequences. He described his high-resolution spectral estimate in terms of a *maximum entropy* formalism in his 1975 doctoral thesis and has been instrumental in the development of modeling approaches to high-resolution spectral estimation. Burg's approach was initially applied to the geophysical exploration for oil and gas through the analysis of seismic waves. The approach is also applicable for technical market analysis because it produces high-resolution spectral estimates using minimal data. This is important because the short-term market cycles are always shifting. Another benefit of the approach is that is maximally responsive to the selected data length and is not subject to distortions due to end effects at the ends of the data. The trading program, MESA, is an acronym for *maximum entropy spectral analysis.*

WHAT IS A CYCLE?

The dictionary definition of a cycle is that it is "an interval or space of time in which is completed one round of events or phenomena that recur regularly and in the same sequence." In the market, we consider a classic cycle exists when the price starts low, rises smoothly to a high over a length of time, and then smoothly falls back to the original price over the same length of time. The time required to complete the cycle is called the *period* of the cycle or the cycle length.

Cycles certainly exist in the market. Many times they are justified on the basis of fundamental considerations. The clearest is the seasonal change for agricultural prices (lowest at harvest), or the decline in real estate prices in the winter. Television analysts are always talking about the rate of inflation being "seasonally adjusted" by the government. But the seasonal is a specific case of the cycle, always being 12 months. Other fundamentals-related cycles can originate from the 18-month cattle-breeding cycle or the monthly cold-storage report on pork bellies.

Business cycles are not as clear, but they exist. Business cycles vary with interest rates. The government sets objectives for economic growth based on its ability to hold inflation to reasonable levels. This growth is increased or decreased by adding or withdrawing funds from the economy and by changing the rate at which government lends money to banks. Easing of rates encourages business; tightening of rates inhibits it. Inevitably this process alternates, causing what we see as a business cycle. Although in practice this cycle may repeat in the same number of years, the exact repetition of the period is not necessary. The business cycle is limited on the upside by the amount of growth the government will allow (usually 3%) and on the downside by moderate negative growth (about −1%), which indicates a recession. The range of the cycle from +3% to −1% is called its *amplitude*.

COMPONENTS OF THE MARKET

Statisticians and economists have identified four important characteristics of price movement. All price forecasts and analyses deal with each of these elements:

1. A *trend*, or a tendency to move in one direction for a specified time period.

2. A *seasonal* factor, a pattern related to the calendar.

3. A *cycle* (other than seasonal) that may exist due to government action, the lag in starting up and winding down of business, or crop estimate announcements.

4. Other unaccountable price movement, often called *noise*.

Since points 2 and 3 are both cycles, it is clear that cycles are a significant and accepted part of all price movement.

When trading using cycles, one key question is the desired time span of the trade. At one extreme, the 54-year Kondratieff economic cycle (not without its critics) could be considered. A cattle rancher might prefer the 18-month breeding cycle, while a grain farmer probably hedges on the basis of the annual harvest. Speculators often work over a short (sometimes very short) time span.

Behavioral cycles in prices have been most popular in Elliotts' wave theory and more recently in the works of Gann. But these methods have a large element of interpretation and subjectivity.

Short-term cycles can exist even within the definition of point 4, "noise." A casual glance at almost any bar chart shows, in retrospect, that short-term cycles ebb and flow. The ability to isolate and use market phenomena, such as cycles, is related to the awareness of its existence and the tools available. Many forecasting methods were not practical until the computer became popular. Now these methods can be used by nearly everyone. The philosophical foundation for these short-term cycles is derived from random walk theory and is developed so you will feel more comfortable dealing with cycles within the constraints of point 4.

RANDOM WALK

Randomness in the market results from a large number of traders exercising their prerogatives with different motivations of profit, loss, greed, fear, and entertainment; it is complicated by different perspectives of time. Market movement can therefore be analyzed in terms of random variables. One such analysis is the random walk. Imagine an atom of oxygen in a plastic box containing nothing but air. The path of this atom is erratic as it bounces from one molecule to another. Brownian motion is used to describe the way the atom moves. Its path is described as a three-dimensional random walk. Following such a random walk, the position of that atom is just as likely to be at any one location in that box as at any other.

Another form of the random walk is more appropriate for describing the motion of the market. This form is a two-dimensional random walk, called the "drunkard's walk." The two-dimensional structure is appropriate for the market because the prices can only go up or down in one dimension. The other dimension, time, can only move forward. These are similar to the way a drunkard's walk is described.

DIFFUSION EQUATION

The drunkard's walk is formulated by allowing the drunkard to step to either the right or left randomly with each step forward.

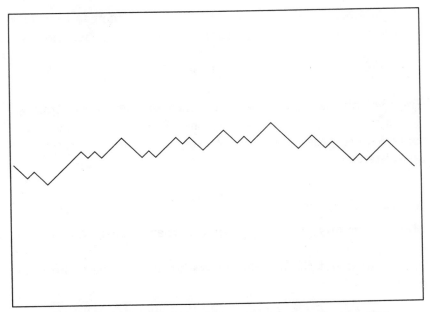

Figure 1–1   Random Walk Path, Direction Is Random Variable

To ensure randomness, the decision to step right or left is made on the outcome of a coin toss from a fair coin. If the coin turns up heads, the drunk steps to the right. If the coin turns up tails, the drunk steps to the left. Viewed from above, we see the random path the drunk has followed. Figure 1–1 shows a computer-generated path using the drunkard's walk rules. We can write a differential equation for this path because the rate change of time is related to the rate change of position in two dimensions.

Differential equations are used to describe relationships due to variations. For example, velocity is the change of distance with respect to time, such as miles per hour. Written as a differential equation, velocity is expressed as

$$V = dx\,/dt$$

so that the equation shows that velocity is the change of distance with respect to time. Think of the d in the equation as meaning the difference. Similarly, acceleration is the change of velocity with respect to time. The equation for acceleration becomes

$$a = dV/dt$$

Since velocity is the change of distance with respect to time we can think of acceleration as being the second rate change of distance with respect to time. Now the equation for acceleration can be written as

$$a = dV/dt = d^2x/dt^2$$

Mathematicians use these formats when writing differential equations.

Writing out the drunkard's walk problem, the differential equation is

$$dP/dt = D * d^2P/dx^2$$

where P = the position in time and space
D = the diffusion constant.

This relatively famous differential equation (among mathematicians, at least) is known as the *diffusion equation*. In words, this equation states that the change of position with respect to time is proportional to the second rate change of position with respect to space. It describes many natural phenomena; for example, the way heat travels up a silver spoon when it's placed in a hot cup of coffee. A better analogy to the way the market works is that the diffusion equation can describe the plume of smoke coming from a smokestack[2]. Figure 1–2 shows 100 overlayed computer-generated drunkard's walk paths. Using some imagination, you can picture Figure 1–2 as a plume of smoke.

Picture this plume of smoke in a gentle breeze. The plume is roughly conical, widening with greater distance from the smokestack. The plume is bent in the direction of the breeze.

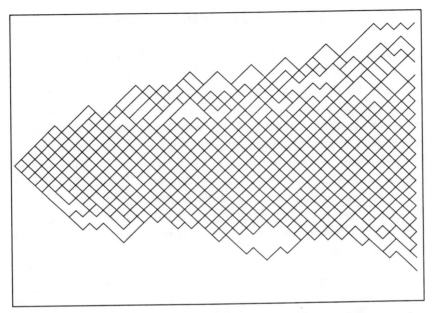

Figure 1-2   100 Random Walk Paths Overlayed, Direction Is Random Variable

The diffusion equation describes the position of a single smoke particle, and you see the random position of all the particles in macrospect. Due to the random nature of the variable, the best estimate of the position you can make for any particle is the average position of the plume. There clearly are no cycles involved. Relating the smoke plume to the market, the general direction can be determined by averaging the random price. This, of course, is the moving average. It identifies the trend as surely as you can see the bending of the smoke plume in the breeze. Several centuries ago Gauss proved that such an average is the best estimator for a truly random variable. Note that the estimation, or prediction, degrades with distance from the origin just as the smoke plume widens as it leaves the smokestack. For this reason, moving average predictors for the market trend to degrade rapidly, as do most forecasts.

TELEGRAPHER'S EQUATION

Let's revisit the mathematical formulation of the drunkard's walk problem. This time, the result of the coin flip will determine whether the drunk takes the next step in the same direction as the previous one or whether he reverses his direction. This makes the random variable his momentum rather than direction. Figure 1–3 shows a computer-generated drunkard's walk path formed using momentum as the random variable. Mathematicians call this the *Continuous Time Random Walk*, or CTRW[3]. In this case the random variable is his momentum rather than his direction. We have altered the way his position changes as a function of time. When we now express his position as a differential equation, we obtain

$$d^2P/dt^2 + (1/T) * dP/dt = C * d^2P/dx^2$$

where T and C are constants.

This is also a famous equation. It is called the *telegrapher's equation* because, among other things, it describes the way the electronic waves travel along a telegraph wire. Note the structure of the telegrapher's equation is identical to the structure of the diffusion equation except it contains the extra term for the second rate change of position with respect to time. The telegrapher's equation also describes the meandering of a river, a physical phenomenon we can relate to the market. Viewed as an aerial photograph, every river in the world meanders. This meandering is due not to a lack of homogeneity in the soil, but to the conservation of energy. You can appreciate that soil homogeneity is not a factor because other streams, such as ocean currents, also meander in a homogeneous medium. Ocean currents are not nearly as familiar to most of us as rivers.

Every meander in a river is independent of other meanders, satisfying the random requirement. If we looked at all the meanders as an ensemble, overlaying one on top of another like a multiple exposure photograph, the meander randomness would also

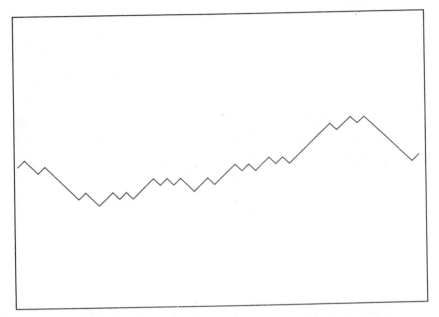

Figure 1-3   Random Walk Path, Random Variable Is Momentum

become apparent. The composite envelope of the river paths would be about the same as the cross section of the smoke plume. Figure 1–4 illustrates this point by showing the overlay of 100 drunkard's walk paths where the random variable is momentum. On the other hand, if we are in a given meander, we are virtually certain of the general path of the river. The result is that the river has a short-term coherency but is random over the longer span.

By analogy, the river meanders are the kind of cycles we have in the market. We can measure and use these short-term cycles to our advantage if we realize they can come and go in the longer term.

We can extend our analogy to understand when short-term cycles occur. The physical reason a river meanders is that it attempts to maintain a constant slope on its way to the ocean. The constant water slope is a variation on the principle of the conservation of energy. If the water speeds up, the width of the river

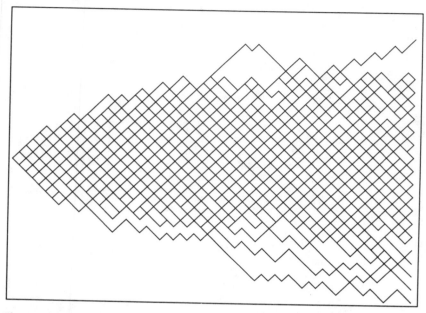

Figure 1–4 100 Random Walk Paths Overlayed, Random Variable Is Momentum

decreases to yield a constant flow volume. The faster flow contains more kinetic energy, and the river attempts to slow it down by changing direction. However, the river direction cannot change abruptly because of the momentum of the flow. Meandering results. Thus, the meanders cause the river to take the path of least resistance in the energy sense. We should think of markets in just the same way. Time must progress as surely as the river must flow to the ocean. The overbought and oversold conditions result from an attempt to conserve the "energy" of the market. This "energy" arises from all the fear and greed emotions of the traders.

You can test the principle of conservation of energy for yourself. Tear a strip about 1 inch wide along the side of a standard sheet of paper about 11 inches long. Grasp each end of this strip between your thumb and forefinger of each hand. Now move your hands together. Your compression is putting energy into this strip, and its natural response can have several forms. These forms are determined by the boundary conditions that you forced. If both hands are pointing up, the response is a single upward arc, approximately one alternation of a sine wave. If both hands are pointing down, the response is a downward arc. If one hand is pointing down and the other is pointing up, the strip response to the energy input is approximately a full sine wave. The four lowest modes are the natural response following the principle of conservation of energy. You can introduce additional bends in the strip, but a minor jiggling will cause the paper to snap to one of the four lowest modes, the exact mode depending on the boundary conditions that you impose.

Tying all this theory together, we can judge that the market will be random if the majority of traders ask themselves "Will the market go up or down?" In this case the random variable is direction. On the other hand, if the majority of traders ask "Will the trend continue?" the random variable is market momentum and a short-term cycle will follow. A trend does not necessarily produce cycles, because the trend can exist and the traders could still be asking themselves if the market is going to be up or down. There is no reliable measure of mass trader psychology leading to cycles. Therefore, we must be content with identifying these short-term cycles as they arise.

CONCLUSIONS

Arguments that cycles exist in the market arise not only from fundamental considerations or direct measurement but also on philosophical grounds related to physical phenomena. The natural response to any physical disturbance is a corrective motion. If you pluck a guitar string, the string vibrates with cycles you can hear. By analogy, we have every right to expect that the market will respond to disturbances with a cyclic motion. This expectation is reinforced with random walk theory that suggests there are times the market prices can be described by the diffusion equation and other times when the market prices can be described by the telegrapher's equation.

The challenge for technical traders is to recognize when the short-term cycles are present and to trade them in a logical and consistent manner so these cycles can contribute profitably to the bottom line.

In the chapters that follow I will define the basics of cycles and how to manipulate them to tune the momentum and moving average functions—components of every technical trading indicator. Cycle primitives will even be related to traditional charting patterns, perhaps giving these patterns a whole new meaning to you. Perhaps most importantly, I will discuss when to use cycles for trading and when to avoid their use.

2

CYCLE BASICS

The one thing on which market technicians agree is that the market varies. Precisely how it varies is the matter of the continuous debate. Each of the technical trading techniques, from classical chart patterns to Elliott's wave, construct a simplified model of the market. Each technique describes the market in terms of the model parameters. The parameters are then adjusted to describe the current market conditions and further used to extrapolate and predict future market activity. Cycle analysis is no different.

Cycles are a simplified technical model of the market. The model is at least as complex as most other models because several cycles can coexist; cycles are often mixed with noise, and all the cycles ebb and flow with time. The primitive component of complex cycles is the sine wave. The sine wave is the natural cycle primitive for several reasons:

1. The sine wave is the mathematically smoothest waveform describing a cycle and harmonic motion.

2. More complicated forms of waves are made up of the sums of simple sine waves.

3. Sine and cosine waves form an independent parameter set for advanced analyses such as Fourier transforms.

Just as with any model, we must define the parameters of the components so that we can assemble them into the logical complex model. The cycle parameters are *frequency, phase,* and *amplitude.*

FREQUENCY

A cycle is any process where a point of observation returns to its origin. One example is a clock pendulum. The pendulum swings with such regularity that it has been used for centuries as the time standard for the clock. Thus, a prime characteristic of a cycle is *frequency.* The rotation of an automobile engine is cyclic. The frequency is the number of revolutions per minute the crankshaft makes. The term *2000 RPM* should be familiar to most motorists. RPM is the acronym for *revolutions per minute.* Each rotation is a cycle, and the period of such a cycle is 1/2000 of a minute. That is, the period of the cycle is the reciprocal of its frequency. In trading we commonly refer to cycles in terms of their period rather than their frequency. For example, the frequency of a 10-day cycle is 0.1 cycles per day.

Think of the automobile engine crankshaft. We will picture a cycle as being generated by a rotating arrow, or vector, connected to the crankshaft. This arrow is called a phasor. The cycle is complete when the tip of the phasor has completed a full rotation to the origin. We can generate the fundamental cycle building block, or primitive, from our rotating arrow. Imagine the tip of the arrow casting a shadow on the vertical axis as if it were illuminated from the right and left by flashlights. The amplitude of this shadow rises and falls as a sine wave with respect to time.

Alternating current generators creating electricity operate much like our phasor. The copper wires on the rotating armature first move parallel to the magnetic lines of the fixed pole pieces, transitioning to cutting across the magnetic lines as the armature rotates. The copper wires moving through the magnetic field create the electric current flow. The resulting voltage and current wave shapes are sine waves. In the United States the AC frequency is standardized at 60 cycles per second.

Frequency is a uniquely singular measurable parameter of a cycle. A simple sine wave can have only one frequency. A sine wave is a *primitive* because we can add sine waves of different frequencies, phases, and amplitudes to create complex wave shapes. A sine wave can be described mathematically in terms of an infinite power series as

$$\sin(x) = x - x^3/3! + x^5/5! - x^7/7! + \ldots$$

where ! denotes the factorial. That is, $5! = 1 * 2 * 3 * 4 * 5$.

The simplified description of the sine wave relative to a power series expansion is another reason to consider it to be a primitive function.

PHASE

Phase relationships of the cycle primitive are important for the understanding of moving average and momentum functions. Moving averages cause lagging phase relationships, and momentum produces leading phases. We will show later how these relationships are combined to form useful indicators.

The relationship between the phasor and the sine wave is shown in Figure 2–1. At time zero the phasor is pointed to the right and the sine wave amplitude is zero. The phasor rotates

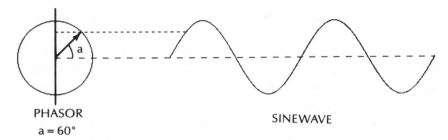

PHASOR
a = 60°

SINEWAVE

Figure 2–1   Phasor Relationship to Sinewave

counterclockwise, so the sine wave rises toward a positive maximum as time progresses. The maximum is reached when the phasor is oriented 90 degrees with respect to the origin (straight up). After the maximum is reached, the phasor rotation carries to 180 degrees (opposite) relative to the origin. The cycle continues to be drawn as the phasor rotates counterclockwise, and continues cycle after cycle. The dotted line shows the relationship of the phasor and the sine wave when the phase angle is approximately 60 degrees.

Another special primitive is called the cosine wave. A negative cosine wave lags the sine wave by 90 degrees in .phase as shown in Figure 2–2. This cosine wave can be generated by a phasor lagging the original phasor by 90 degrees. Note that when the cosine wave is a maximum, the sine wave has a zero value that corresponds to the rate of change at that point. When the negative cosine wave goes through zero from negative to positive

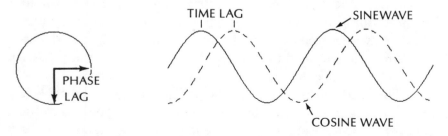

TIME LAG   SINEWAVE

PHASE
LAG

COSINE WAVE

Figure 2–2   Phase Relationship of Sine and Cosine Waves

values, it has the maximum rate of change and this is just where the sine wave has its maximum amplitude. The sine wave has its largest negative value just when the negative cosine wave crosses through zero from positive to negative and its negative rate change is maximum. Thus, Figure 2–2 qualitatively shows that the rate change of a negative cosine wave is a sine wave and the rate change of a sine wave is just a cosine wave.

AMPLITUDE

Amplitude is the strength or "power" of the cycle. Power is independent of frequency and phase. The size of a light bulb in your house is, perhaps, 60 watts. This is the rating for the power it consumes to generate light. The power has no phase angle and is independent of the 60 cycle frequency of the voltage on your lines. In fact the power is proportional to the square of the voltage due to a physical law called Ohm's law. Squaring the voltage phasor means multiplying it by itself in the same direction, regardless of the phase angle. Thus, the phase angle has no meaning in the definition of power.

It is important to note that the power of a cycle is proportional to the square of its wave amplitude. If one wave is 1.414 (square root of 2) times larger than another, this wave will have twice the power.

Power can vary over a wide range, and we often want to look at the low-amplitude signals at the same time that we look at the high-amplitude signals. One way to do this is to look at the power of the signals on a logarithmic scale to achieve the amplitude compression. If we take a given power as a reference, then a signal having twice the power has a logarithmic ratio of 0.3. A signal power four times larger has a logarithmic ratio of 0.6, twice the value of the previous ratio. When the signal power is 10 times larger, the logarithmic ratio is 1.0. The numbers repeat for each tenfold increase in power. For example, the logarithm of 20 is 1.3.

Power is often expressed in terms of *deciBels*. The *Bel* is named after Alexander Graham Bell for the research he performed on audio power to help the deaf. A Bel is just the logarithm of a power ratio. *Deci-* is a prefix meaning one tenth. Therefore, a deciBel is one tenth of the logarithm of a power ratio. The power ratios can be both larger and smaller than unity. If the power ratio is less than one, the sign of the logarithm is negative. For example, a power ratio of 0.5 is equivalent to −3 dB and a power ratio of 0.01 is equivalent to −20 dB. Recalling that the square of the wave amplitude is proportional to power, we can calculate that −6 dB means that the wave amplitude is half the amplitude of the reference wave.

It is common practice in spectrum analysis to compare all the cycle amplitudes with the amplitude of the strongest signal. Therefore, the strongest signal has a power of zero dB because it is being compared with itself (the logarithm of 1 is zero), and all other signals have powers measured in negative deciBels.

3

PRINCIPLES OF CYCLES

Traditional charting is an analytical technique that is difficult to master because of the large number of rules associated with the chart patterns. The charts are laboriously prepared and often look as if they were works of art. The beauty of cycle analysis is that it cuts through all these rules by describing the market action in terms of primitives. Once you understand the cyclic activity, the result of combinations of the primitives will become clear to you.

All market chart formations can be described in terms of only three principles of cycles:

1. Principle of proportionality.

2. Principle of superposition.

3. Principle of resonance.

PRINCIPLE OF PROPORTIONALITY

The *principle of proportionality* is simply that the cycle amplitudes are in proportion to the selected time scale. Figures 3–1

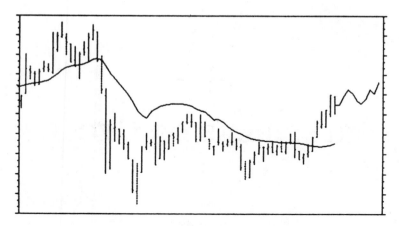

Figure 3–1   Weekly or Daily Chart?

and 3–2 represent the bar charts for the same commodity with the time and price scales removed. Which is the weekly chart and which is the daily chart? You simply can't tell by casual observation because of the principle of proportionality. This principle has also become an important factor in the more recent fractal mathematics.

Another way to convince yourself that the principle of proportionality holds is to assume that it doesn't, and then test the

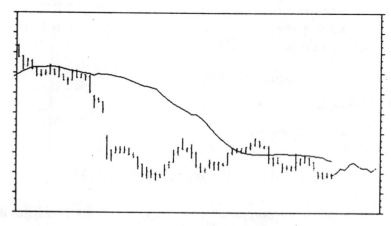

Figure 3–2   Weekly or Daily Chart?

result. Suppose we had wild hourly swings that far exceeded the day-to-day variations. If that were true, the daily charts would have a virtually horizontal average and the daily ranges would fill the chart. This clearly is not the case, and so the failure of the assumption validates the principle of proportionality.

PRINCIPLE OF SUPERPOSITION

The *principle of superposition* asserts that we can build complex shapes from the primitive building blocks. If you have ever watched waves on the water, you have seen the total wave action is the summation of waves from several sources. For example, the wake of a boat combines with wind-driven waves to lap at the dock.

We can use the cycle primitives to synthesize more complex wave shapes. Suppose we start with a sine wave whose angular frequency is w and subtract from it another sine wave at twice the frequency at half amplitude. Then we add another sine wave at three times the frequency with one third the amplitude. The three primitive sine wave components are shown in Figure 3–3, and the resulting composite waveform is shown in Figure 3–4.

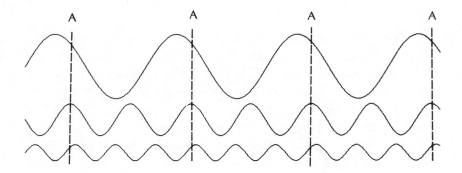

$$Wave = \sin(w * t) - (1/2) * \sin(2 * w * t) + (1/3) * \sin(3 * w * t)$$

Figure 3–3 Individual Components of a Sawtooth Waveform

Wave = sin(w * t) − (¹/₂) * sin(2 * w * t) + (¹/₃) * sin(3 * w * t)

Figure 3–4 Sawtooth Waveform Synthesized from First Three Sinewave Components

The waves are nearly in phase at the points marked *A,* while they add and subtract differently at other parts of the cycle. The composite waveform repeats with the period of the fundamental frequency because all the components are harmonically related (their frequency is an integer multiple of the fundamental frequency). The composite repeats itself cycle after cycle.

The mathematical expression for the Figure 3–4 composite waveform is

$$\text{Wave} = \sin(w * t) - (\tfrac{1}{2}) * \sin(2 * w * t) + (\tfrac{1}{3}) * \sin(3 * w * t)$$

where w = the angular frequency of the fundamental
t = the time variable.

We could continue to add cycle primitives using a continuation of the sequence, alternately adding and subtracting the next harmonic at an amplitude that is the reciprocal of its harmonic number. If we continued the sequence to infinity, the resultant waveform would be the sawtooth shown in Figure 3–5. Such an infinite series of harmonic sine waves to describe a complex wave shape is called a *Fourier series.* In the case of the sawtooth, the waveform compromises only two straight lines over a complete cycle.

It is easy to get carried away with analysis. The equations for the straight lines in a sawtooth are simple. Describing the

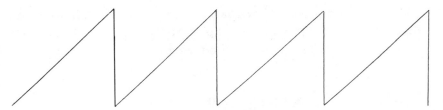

Figure 3–5 Perfect Sawtooth Waveform (Infinite Fourier Series)

sawtooth in terms of cycles, we have an infinite Fourier series. In turn, each sine wave can be described as an infinite power series, making analysis untenable. The point is that we must always use the right tool for the job. If we want to approximately describe a waveform in terms of its measurable cycle primitives, then cycles are the right tool to use.

The cycle primitives do not have to be harmonically related. For example, the common biorhythms are just the superposition of 28-, 30-, and 32-day sine waves. Mystical powers are often attributed to this superposition of nonharmonic sine waves. The patterns appear to be unique because true repetition occurs only about every 10 years, the product of the lowest common factors of their cycle periods.

In another example of complex waves closer to trading, followers of the Elliott wave theory describe the market in terms of five waves. Figure 3–4 is repeated as Figure 3–6, marked to show the five waves. Viewed from this perspective,

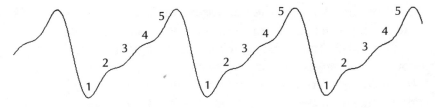

$$\text{Wave} = \sin(w * t) - (1/2) * \sin(2 * w * t) + (1/3) * \sin(3 * w * t)$$

Figure 3–6 Elliott Waves Inferred by Synthesis of a Sawtooth Waveform from the First Three Terms of the Fourier Series

Elliotticians embrace cycle theory and even the principle of proportionality in their more complex analyses. I prefer to think of the market only in terms of the measurable primitives.

PRINCIPLE OF RESONANCE

Have you ever strummed a stretched rubber band and watched it oscillate? Have you ever held a ruler over the edge of a desk, pulled down on the loose end, and released it to watch the ruler vibrate? These are two examples of *resonance*. The items oscillate at a frequency determined by the restoring forces and the boundary conditions. The maximum excursions of the oscillations can be described as a standing wave.

When you throw a pebble into a pond of still water, the waves travel outward until they strike an object like a wall, whereupon they are reflected. Much the same thing happens with resonance. When you deflect the ruler you put energy into it. The wave travels down the ruler when you release it, but there is no place for the energy to go when the wave reaches the desk, and so the wave is reflected back. The wave now travels toward the free end, causing it to move. But when the wave reaches the free end there is no place for the energy to go, and so it is reflected back again. The process continues with waves traveling in both directions on the ruler. The forward and back waves combine to form the standing wave that you see as the maximum excursion of the ruler. The same effect occurs with the rubber band except the boundary conditions hold both ends fixed so that the maximum excursion occurs at the center.

Here's how the standing wave works. Figure 3–7 shows both a forward wave and backward wave. Necessarily, these waves have the same period because they have the same frequency. As shown, the two waves are in phase at point *A* and are out of phase at point *B*. Imagine time progressing so the 90-degree point on the forward wave arrives at the fixed point *A*. The 90-degree point of the backward wave arrives at the fixed point *A* simultaneously

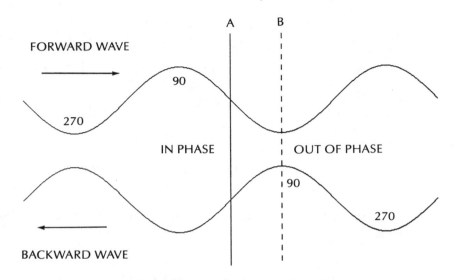

Figure 3–7   Traveling Waves

with that of the forward wave so that the effects of the two waves at point *A* are additive. Because both waves arrive at point *A* in phase throughout the cycle, the additive action is independent of time. In exactly the same way, the forward wave and backward wave are always out of phase at point *B*, and the two waves cancel each other independently of time.

The only reason that the standing waves diminish with time is because energy is lost to audio energy or to molecular frictional energy in the rubber band or ruler. The standing waves are determined by the inherent restoring forces and by the boundary conditions.

Figure 3–8 depicts the kind of wave shape that can result from the principle of resonance. The lower frequency envelope is the standing wave. A higher frequency (in this case) moves through the envelope as a traveling wave because it is not subject to the same boundary conditions as a lower frequency standing wave. That is, its energy is transferred into the future or absorbed rather than being reflected. In this way, the lower

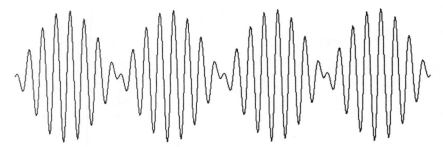

Figure 3–8   Low Frequency Standing Wave Modulation

frequency standing wave modulates the amplitude of the higher frequency.

SYNTHESIZED CHART PATTERNS

We can synthesize a wide variety of chart patterns using only the three principles of proportionality, superposition, and resonance. Analysis is the inverse operation of synthesis, so that if we understand synthesis we have a greater insight into analysis techniques and procedures. While synthesis is relatively easy, analysis is very difficult because of the wide range of parameter combinations that must be accommodated. We often perform analysis by making simplifying assumptions and then testing these assumptions.

Trading Channels

Trading channels are synthesized using the principles of proportionality and superposition. We use the following three primitives:

1. Trend (a piece of a large amplitude long cycle).

2. Medium-length cycle of medium amplitude.

3. Short-term cycle of small amplitude.

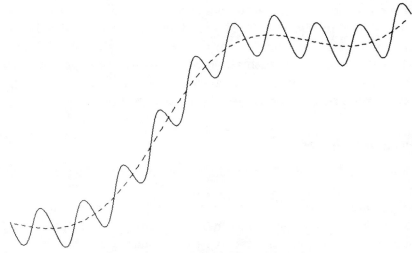

Figure 3–9   Synthesized Trading Channel

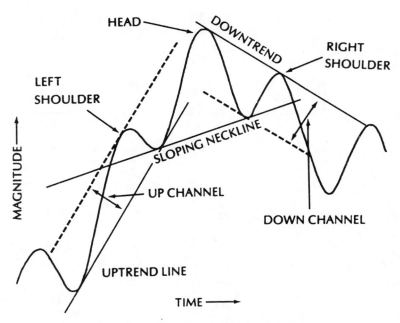

Figure 3–10   Head-and-Shoulders Pattern

When we add these three components, the resultant is the wave-form shown in Figure 3–9. The trading channels are simply the maximum and minimum excursions of the short-term cycle when it is combined with the other two cycle components. In this case the "channel" is bent with the medium-length cycle rather than being constructed from straight lines.

Head and Shoulders

One of the favorite formations of the chartists is the classic head-and-shoulders pattern shown in Figure 3–10. Each of the chart characteristics are noted on the figure. Conventional interpretation would have the downside break through the sloping neckline confirming the trend reversal called by the previous breakthrough of the uptrend line. Even the return move followed by further downside activity is indicated.

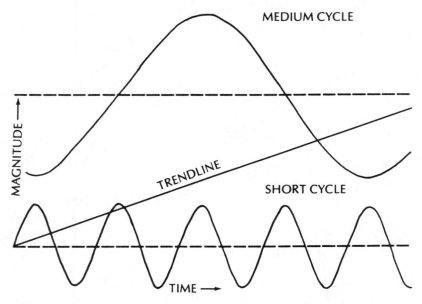

Figure 3–11   Cyclic Components of Head-and-Shoulders Pattern

Now, let's see how we synthesized that head-and-shoulders pattern. Figure 3–11 shows the primitive components of the composite wave shape. We simply used the principle of superposition and added a trend line (a segment of a very long cycle), a medium-length cycle, and a short-term cycle at half the amplitude and four times the frequency. The short-term cycle and the medium-length cycle phase together at their peaks to form the head. The two shoulders are formed basically by the short cycle adding to the medium-length cycle at its midpoint.

Knowing the cyclic components makes analysis far easier. We would establish the long-term trend directly. The medium trend and its breakpoint are established by the medium-length cycle. The short-term cycle gives the best entry points for trades to be made in the direction of the medium-length trend. It is clear that the probability of a profitable trade is best if you enter using the short-term cycle with the trade in the direction

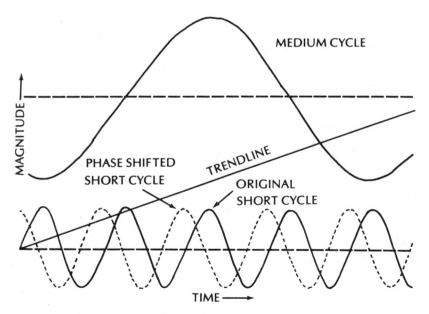

Figure 3–12   Relative Phase of Shifted Short Cycle

of the medium cycle. Trades where the two cycles conflict in direction should be avoided. That's about all there is to it, using the primitives. No complicated rules to learn, just trade the cycles you measure.

Double Top

What happens to the chart pattern of Figure 3–10 if we simply leftshift the phase of the short cycle by 120 degrees? This case is shown in Figure 3–12, where the original phase of the short cycle is shown as the solid line and the shifted phase as the dotted line. Now when we invoke the principle of superposition, the peaks of the short cycle add to the medium cycle on either side of its peak. The result is the double top pattern of Figure 3–13.

Using cyclic analysis and knowing the primitive components, there is no change in our trading strategy. We still enter on the turning points of the short term cycle in the direction of

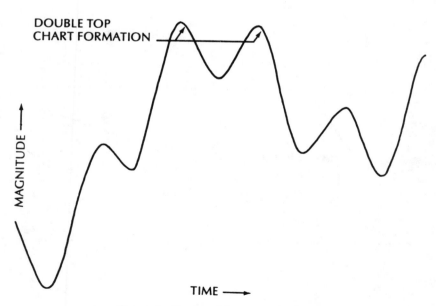

Figure 3–13   Double Top Formation

the medium length cycle. There are no new rules to learn, and we treat a double top formation exactly the same way we treat a head-and-shoulders formation.

Flags and Pennants

All these chart patterns are characterized by the top and bottom envelopes of the price action not being parallel, as opposed to the parallel boundaries of a trading channel. The schematic of a typical pennant is shown in Figure 3–14. Conventional wisdom has the price continuing in the same direction after the flag as it was before the flag occurred. This may or may not be true, and we can quickly isolate when it will be true using cycles.

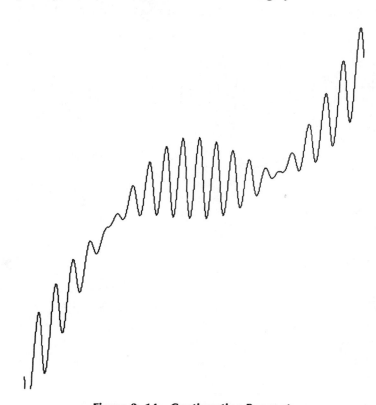

Figure 3–14   Continuation Pennant

Figure 3–8 shows a nonparallel envelope due to the principle of resonance. If we now invoke the principle of superposition and the principle of proportionality, we can generate the pennant by adding a trend, a medium-length cycle traveling wave, and a short term cycle modulated by the medium-length cycle standing wave. Using these components depicted in Figure 3–15, the conventional wisdom prevails and the price rise continues after the pennant.

However, if we double the length of the medium-length cycle and double its amplitude (principle of proportionality) and eliminate the trendline, the primitive components of the pennant are shown in Figure 3–16. In this case, the price reverses after the pennant because the trend is replaced with the stronger cycle. The schematic of the total price is shown in Figure 3–17. We still

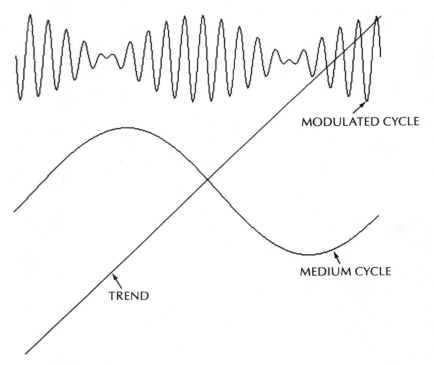

Figure 3–15   Primitive Components of a Continuation Pennant

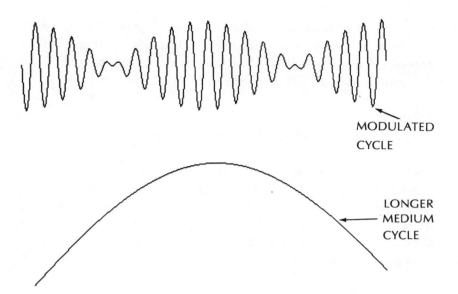

MODULATED
CYCLE

LONGER
MEDIUM
CYCLE

Figure 3–16   Primitive Components of a Reversal Pennant

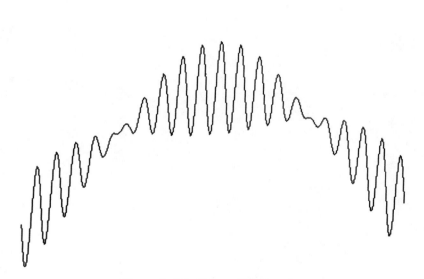

Figure 3–17   Reversal Pennant

have virtually the same pennant we had in Figure 3–14, but reading the pennant as a continuation signal is dead wrong. Had we known the cycle primitives, the price direction at the end of the flag could have easily been predicted.

FOR FURTHER STUDY

The relationship between chart patterns and cycles has enough variations that this topic can be the basis of an entire book by itself. The goal in this chapter was only to make you aware that the relationships exist and that you can use cycles to aid your charting analysis. J. M. Hurst[1] is recommended for further reading on the subject.

4

EFFECTS OF
MOVING AVERAGES

SIMPLE MOVING AVERAGES

Several hundred years ago Karl Friedrich Gauss proved that the average is the best estimator of a random variable. As a result, in statistics the mean is always the nominal forecast. This best estimator is certainly true for the market in the case where the diffusion equation applies. The best estimate of the location of the smoke plume is the center of the plume, the average across its width. This is probably the reason moving averages are heavily used by technical traders—they want the best estimator of the random variable.

An *N-day simple average* is formed by adding the prices over N days and dividing by N. The simple average becomes a moving average by adding the next day's weighted price to the sum and dropping off the weighted first day's price. Thus the simple average "moves" from day to day.

Let's look at how simple moving averages (SMA) behave with cycles. With reference to Figure 4–1, we will take an average

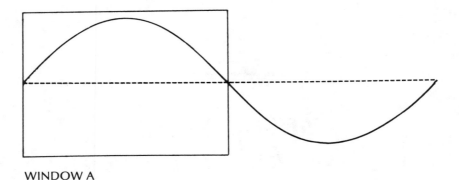

WINDOW A

Figure 4–1   Half Cycle Average Window

of all the sampled points of the sine wave in window A. Window A covers half a cycle. If the window were wider, it would include some negative values of the sine wave and the peak value of the moving average would be reduced. On the other hand, if the window were narrower, all values in the positive alternation would not be included in the window. Therefore, a simple moving average of half the cycle length has special significance.

Referencing the moving average to the right-hand side of the window, the moving average is maximum at point A in Figure 4–2. As we move the window to the right in our mind's eye, we start to include some negative values of the sine wave in the moving average. Therefore, the moving average amplitude declines. When the right-hand edge of the window reaches position B, there are just as many negative values inside the window as positive values. The result is that the moving average has a zero value at position B. We can continue to move the window, creating the moving average shown as the dashed line.

We can make some observations about a half-cycle moving average of a sine wave. First, the shape of the moving average is a negative cosine wave. From the phasor discussion in Chapter 2, you recognize that the half-cycle moving average lags the sine wave by exactly 90 degrees. The trendline for the sine wave is zero, so we can observe that the sine wave price function reaches

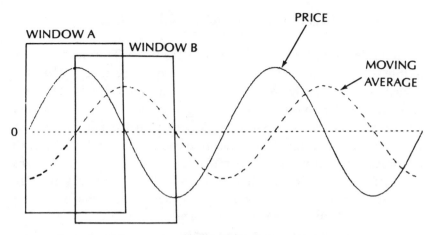

Figure 4-2 Half Cycle Moving Average

its maximum just as the half-cycle moving average crosses the trendline from bottom to top. Similarly, the price function just reaches its valley as the half-cycle moving average crosses the trendline from top to bottom.

Another special simple moving average is one taken over the full period of the cycle. In this case there are just as many positive values in the window as negative values. The result is that this moving average is always zero, regardless of the phase angle position of the window. If the price consists of a trendline plus the sine wave, the full-cycle moving average removes the cycle part and retains the trendline.

The action of the half-cycle and full-cycle moving averages suggests a trading system. You would sell when the half-cycle moving average crosses the full-cycle moving average from bottom to top because this is where the sine wave has its peak value. You would buy when the half-cycle moving average crosses the full-cycle moving average from top to bottom because this is where the sine wave has its lowest value. Note that these trading rules are exactly the opposite of the rules for short and long moving averages in trend-following systems.

MOVING AVERAGES AS FILTERS

A moving average is basically a *low pass filter*. That is, the averaging smooths the input data. This smoothing means that the higher frequency wiggles (noise) are removed and only the lower frequency components (bigger moves) are allowed to pass. The smoothing action uses historical data so that the filtered output is always delayed in phase relative to the input. We have already examined the filter characteristic of two special low pass filters, the half-cycle moving average and the full-cycle moving average. We can establish a more general picture of the passband and delay characteristics of the moving average.

Another way to view the averaging window is as a multiplier in the time domain. The sampled data are multiplied by one for all values inside the window and are multiplied by zero for all values outside the window. In the case of continuous time, the multiplier is a rectangular pulse of unit amplitude in the time domain. The Fourier transform of a rectangular function like the multiplier is $\sin(X)/X$, where X is a generalized frequency variable. The frequency response is the Fourier transform of the time function, so the frequency response of the moving average is just $\sin(X)/X$. This $\sin(X)/X$ function first goes to zero when $X = $ Pi (Pi = 3.14159). We also know the filter response is zero when the window length is a full cycle. Equating these two conditions, we find that

$$X = \text{Pi} * \textit{(cycle period/window length)}$$

The filter has a zero response each time the cycle period is a multiple of the window length because there are as many positive values as negative values of the sine wave within the window. The amplitude response of the simple moving average low pass filter is shown in Figure 4–3.

The value of $\sin(X)/X$ approaches unity as X approaches zero because $\sin(X)$ is approximately equal to X for small values of X. Therefore, very low-frequency components such as

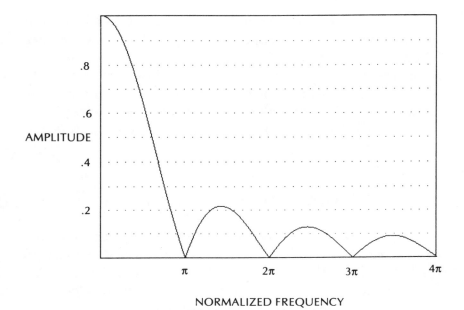

NORMALIZED FREQUENCY

Figure 4-3   SMA Frequency Response

trendlines are passed through the filter virtually unattenuated. In the special case of the half-cycle moving average, the numerator of the moving average filter is unity because Pi/2 radians is equal to 90 degrees. The denominator is just Pi/2, and since this value is in the denominator, the filter response is its reciprocal, 2/Pi = .637. That is, the filtered amplitude of a sine wave signal whose period is half the window length will be .637 times the amplitude of the sine wave. The $\sin(X)/X$ functions allow us to calculate the filtered amplitude of any signal as a function of the ratio of its period to the averaging window length.

The phase response of a simple average is linear. We know that a half-cycle moving average is delayed by 90 degrees. From the linearity condition, we know that a quarter-cycle moving average is delayed by 45 degrees and so forth. The shorter the moving average relative to the cycle period the less lag will be induced. Of course, you also get less filtering but that's how filters and Mother Nature work.

Filters can be designed to have a much sharper frequency cutoff than the $\sin(X)/X$ response of the simple moving average. Higher order filters can be designed[1]; however, the use of these filters is discouraged. The amount of delay experienced by a filter is directly related to the order of the filter. In general, the phase response is more important to traders than the frequency attenuation response. Therefore, these higher order filters are not very useful for traders.

EXPONENTIAL MOVING AVERAGES

The *exponential moving average (EMA)* is a way of recursively calculating the average, emphasizing most recent data more than older data. The EMA, by the way, is a mathematical realization of real filters. Simple averages can only be calculated, they cannot be generated in physically realizable filters. The equation for the EMA is

$$\text{NEW EMA} = (1 - (K) * (\text{OLD EMA}) + K * (\text{NEW SAMPLE})$$

where K is a constant < 1.

In words, this equation says that today's EMA is formed by taking a fraction of today's data and adding it to the compliment of the fraction multiplying yesterday's EMA. The equation is convergent when K is less than one because if the data input becomes constant, the value of the EMA approaches that constant. Consider the case where all the new samples are unity. The EMA starts with a zero value, and gradually builds up to almost unity. When this occurs the equation for the NEW EMA is approximately

$$\text{NEW EMA} = (1 - K) + K = 1$$

Since the EMA is a kind of moving average, it is also a low pass filter. A common way to characterize filters is by their *impulse response*. An impulse is a mathematical function that is infinitely high and has zero width. The height approaches infinity and the width approaches zero in such a way that the area of the conceptual rectangle is unity. Applying the impulse to the input of a filter is similar to striking a bell and listening for it to ring out. The impulse function is zero everywhere in time except at time equal zero.

Consider multiplying the impulse by $1/K$, and using this value of the impulse to be the input to our EMA filter. We will assess the impulse response of the EMA using discrete time intervals. The initial output of the EMA filter is unity because there is no old EMA. The EMA1 after the first sample is $(1 - K)$ because the old EMA value was unity and there is no new sample. Similarly EMA2 is $(1 - K)^2$ because the old EMA value was $(1 - K)$ and there is no new sample. As shown in Figure 4–4, the

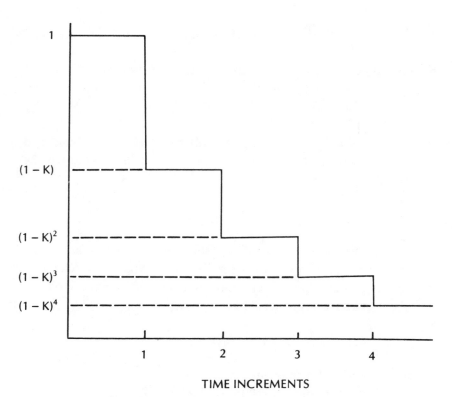

Figure 4–4 EMA Filter Impulse Response

decay of the response to the impulse falls as the exponent of the trial. That is, the EMA has an exponential decay. Now it's easy to see how the exponential moving average got its name. The rate of the decay depends on the K factor.

We can derive the equivalence between an EMA and a SMA using a specific value of K. To do this, we first equate the finite impulse response to an exponential for the Nth sample as

$$(1 - K)^N = \exp(-a * N)$$

where a is a constant to be found.

Taking the natural logarithm of both sides of this equation, we have

$$N * \ln(1 - K) = -a * N$$
$$\ln(1 - K) = -a$$

Expanding the natural logarithm to an infinite series we have

$$\ln(1 - K) = -K - K^2/2 - K^3/3 - K^4/4 - \ldots.$$

When K is small, we can ignore all but the first term, and equating $\ln(1 - K)$ in the preceding two equations, we have the result that

$$K = a$$

Since N is proportional to time, the impulse response of the EMA filter is just $e(-Kt)$. The Fourier transform (the frequency response) of an exponential function, normalized for unity transfer response at zero frequency, is

$$H(W) = K/(K + jW)$$

where $W = 2 * \text{Pi} * \text{frequency}$
$j = $ imaginary operator, a 90-degree shift
$H(W) = 1/(1 + jW/K)$.

We note that the X in the $\sin(X)/X$ SMA function is Pi times the frequency times the SMA period. In the EMA frequency response the variable is $2 * $Pi times the frequency normalized to K. Equating the frequency variables, we have

$$\text{Pi} * F * \text{Window} = 2 * \text{Pi} * F/K$$

Performing the algebra, we obtain the result that

$$K = 2/\text{Window}$$

The amplitude response of the EMA as a function of frequency is compared with the amplitude response of the SMA in Figure 4–5. Equivalence between the SMA and EMA is subject to definition. For example, if we force the amplitude response of the two filters to be the same when half the cycle period is equal

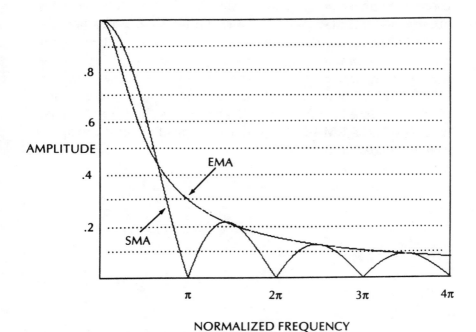

NORMALIZED FREQUENCY

Figure 4–5 EMA/SMA Frequency Response Comparison

to the window length, then the relationship for the EMA K factor is approximately

$$K = 2.5/\text{Window}$$

Hutson[2] derived the relationship between the EMA K factor and the SMA window length as

$$K = 2/(\text{Window} + 1)$$

This definition is based on the average age of each. Note that this definition is substantially the same as the first definition derived except for the shortest window lengths.

Examination of the $H(jW)$ frequency response gives insight into the phase delay of an EMA. When the frequency is near zero, jW/K is much smaller than unity and can be ignored. In this case the output is almost the same as the input, and there is no phase delay. On the other hand, when the frequency approaches infinity, jW/K is much larger than unity and the unity factor in the denominator can be ignored. When this is done, the denominator has a 90-degree phase shift due to the imaginary operator. An interesting result is that the phase lag of an EMA is never more than 90 degrees at any frequency. Since the phase lag of an EMA is always less than the phase lag of an SMA, the EMA is the preferred type of moving average in many applications.

5

EFFECTS OF MOMENTUM

MOMENTUM DEFINED

In the jargon of technical analysis, *momentum* is the rate of change, usually applied to price. It has nothing to do with the length of time to bring a moving body to rest under constant force (the mechanical definition). Nor does the momentum of technical traders imply impetus, as used in the common vernacular.

The summations of moving averages can be viewed as parallels to integrals in the calculus. Since momentum functions are rate of change, they can be viewed as derivatives in the calculus using the same parallels. While not rigorous, this viewpoint allows us to think of momentum as the opposite of moving averages. For example, when moving averages cause a phase delay, momentum functions can introduce a phase lead. We can use this viewpoint to manipulate combinations of moving averages and momentums to generate indicators that will perform to our specifications. That is, we gain an insight on how to adapt our tools to the current market conditions.

While the prospect of a leading phase function can be exciting because of predictive properties for cyclic behavior,

Mother Nature strikes again and does not allow us this luxury without some difficulty. The price data that technical analysts use are noisy. Momentum amplifies this noise, often so much that useful indications are completely obscured. Figure 5–1, showing successive rates of change, demonstrates why the noise is amplified.

The initial curve is a *ramp* and is shown in Figure 5–1a. The "origin" is at the center, so the ramp has a zero slope to the left of the origin and a finite constant slope to the right of the origin. When we take the rate of change of the ramp, we obtain the *step function,* Figure 5–1b. The rate change of the ramp is zero to the left of the origin and instantly jumps to a constant value to the right of the origin, producing the step. Notice that the step appears to be more discontinuous than the ramp. When we take the rate of the step, it has a zero rate of change both to the right and left of the origin. There is only a change exactly at the origin, and this change is infinite because it occurs over a zero horizontal span. This infinite change is

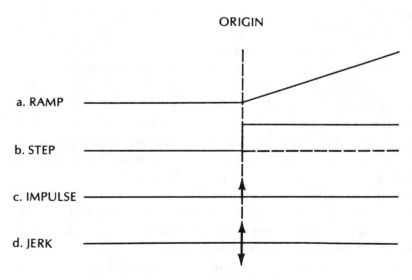

Figure 5–1 Successive Momentum Functions

called an impulse, the same function we used with exponential moving averages (EMAs) in Chapter 4. The *impulse* is shown as Figure 5–1c. Mathematically, the impulse has infinite height and zero width such that the area within this theoretical rectangle is unity. Clearly, the impulse is more discontinuous than the step function. We produce the *jerk* of Figure 5–1d when we take the rate of change of the impulse. The rate of change is zero everywhere except exactly at the origin. The rate of change of the impulse is infinite positive when we "travel up" the front of the conceptual rectangle and infinite negative when we "travel down" the back side of the rectangle. Again, the jerk is more discontinuous than the impulse.

What becomes evident from the example of Figure 5–1 is that momentum is *always* more discontinuous than the original function. Noise in the original data is manifest in the degree of discontinuity. Less noisy data are smoother. If we use momentum without consideration of the impact on noise, we can easily be disappointed in the result. However, properly implemented, we can exploit the phase-leading characteristic when the market is in the cyclic mode.

MOMENTUM LEADING PHASE

Figure 5–2 depicts price as the solid sine wave. When we examine its rate of change, we note that it is zero where the price has its peak and its valley. Further, the maximum positive rate of change occurs just as the price crosses through zero from negative to positive, and the maximum negative rate of change occurs just as the price crosses through zero from positive to negative. The resulting momentum of the sine wave price is shown as the dashed line. Figure 5–2 shows that the momentum of the sine wave price *leads* the price by 90 degrees. We would get approximately the same result if we quantized the continuous sine wave in discrete samples similar to daily data, and took the day-to-day differences to generate the momentum.

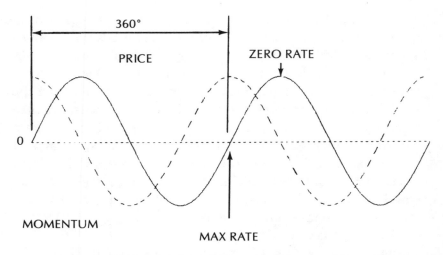

Figure 5–2 Momentum of a Sinewave

When we properly account for the amplitude differences between the sine wave price and its momentum, Figure 5–2 suggests the beginning of a trading system. Each time the momentum crosses the price we have an advance notice of the turning point of the price. This advance notice allows us to establish cycle mode trades with entry and exit points exactly at the peak and valleys of the sine wave without waiting for the crests actually to occur. The difference in timing is crucial toward making successful trades using short-term cycles in the market.

MINIMIZING MOMENTUM NOISE

We can minimize the effects of noise by averaging before we evaluate the momentum. The averaging smooths the price function, so that taking the momentum of the smoothed function is less discontinuous. As an example, a 4-day simple moving average (SMA) using letters to designate the individual prices is

$$SMA1 = (a + b + c + d)/4$$

The 4-day SMA for the next day is

$$SMA2 = (b + c + d + e)/4$$

If we take the simple 1-day momentum of the two moving averages, we obtain

$$Momentum = SMA2 - SMA1$$

$$= (e - a)/4$$

The result is that a simple 1-day momentum of two 4-day SMAs is exactly the same as a 4-day momentum within a constant value of the averaging period. We can extend the logic to the general case that an N-day momentum is exactly the same as the simple momentum of two N-day moving averages.

In the case of the sine wave it is natural to question what happens if we take a half-cycle momentum because this length has the maximum separation between the peak and valley of the sine wave. Such a momentum is the equivalent of taking a half-cycle SMA and then taking the simple momentum of that SMA. The half-cycle SMA introduces a 90-degree phase lag in the form of a negative cosine wave, as we described in Chapter 4. The simple momentum of the half-cycle SMA introduces a 90-degree phase lead, with the result that the final curve is exactly back in phase with the original price function. All the work of performing a half-cycle momentum has produced a curve that has no advantage toward making a trade.

Of course, we can use different N-day momentums to obtain a leading function for the sine wave. For example, a quarter-cycle momentum is equivalent to the simple momentum of a quarter-cycle SMA. The quarter-cycle SMA has only a 45-degree phase lag; the simple momentum has a 90-degree phase lead; the result is a 45-degree phase-leading function. The penalty for this leading function is that the smoothing accomplished by the shorter moving average is not adequate to overcome the added noise of the momentum. We therefore have a trade-off of the leading function and the increased noisiness of that function. If the price data are relatively noise-free, the benefits of the leading-phase function often outweigh the negatives of increase noise.

All successful indicators weigh the balance of smoothing and leading phase in their generation. Recognizing this, you can dissect the indicators and tune them so you can optimally adapt your trading strategy and tactics to the current market.

6

How Cycles
Help Trading

INDICATORS

Some of the more popular trading indicators examine specific aspects of the price function, using combinations of moving average and momentum functions. These indicators usually include the time parameter in their specific names, such as a "14-day RSI" or a "5-period stochastic." The character of the market is always changing and therefore no single fixed indicator best fits all market conditions.

We can classify the varying market by the measured cycles. Since we have an appreciation of the effects of moving average and momentum functions on the phase lead and lag of cycles, the cycle perspective can be used to adapt the indicators to the current market conditions.

The sections that follow discuss how best to adapt RSI (relative strength index), stochastics, and MACD (moving average convergence-divergence) to market cyclic conditions.

RELATIVE STRENGTH INDEX (RSI)

J. Welles Wilder describes the *relative strength index* (RSI) in his book *New Concepts in Technical Trading Systems*[1] as

$$RSI = 1 - 1/(1 + RS)$$

where $RS = CU/CD$
$= $ (14-day averages of closes up)/(14-day average of closes down).

With a little algebra this simplifies to

$$RSI = RS/(1 + RS)$$

$$= CU/(CU + CD)$$

The "closes up" and "closes down" are simple momentums of successive closing prices. The original definition of RSI took the observation period over 14 days. This rigid definition of RSI is what attracted me to investigate technical analysis with the perspective of adapting the indicators to market conditions. Since cycles are one of the few things about market price that can be measured and that can have a short-term predictive capability, I decided cycles would be the focus of my technical analysis research.

In the case of a perfect sine wave of closing prices, the "closes up" would have a maximum value near the center point of the upswing of the cycle and the "closes down" would have a maximum value near the center point of the downswing (see Figure 5–2). Both the "closes up" and "closes down" have a zero value near the peak and valley of the sine wave price. Thus, each of the components has a 90-degree leading characteristic. When these components are averaged over some period, the average introduces phase lag. If the averaging period is exactly a half cycle of the sine wave, the "closes up" and "closes down" are

both exactly in phase with the sine wave price. Since all components of the RSI are in phase with price when the averaging
period is a half cycle, the RSI is also exactly in phase with the
price under this condition. The RSI swings between zero and
one as a perfect sine wave, as shown in Figure 6–1. We can see
the logic of this because at the end of the half-cycle upswing
there are no closes down, and the value of the RSI is one. At the
end of the half-cycle downswing there are no closes up, and the
value of the RSI is zero.

The most simple *BUY* indication from the RSI is when the
RSI swings below 30 percent and crosses back up through
the 30 percent level. Conversely, the *SELL* indication occurs
when the RSI swings above the 70 percent level and then crosses

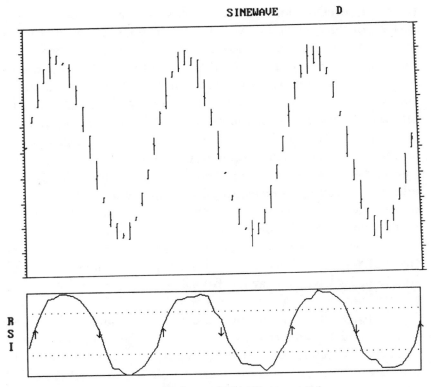

Figure 6–1 RSI for a 20 Day Sinewave Price

back through it. This is not a particularly good strategy for short cycles. For example, on a 10-day cycle it takes two days from the minimum value to identify a crossing of the 30 percent level. You enter the long position trade on the third day. But the entire move occurs in only 5 days, the half cycle of the 10-day cycle. Since you would also exit the trade late, about the best you could hope for is to break even. This is not true when the RSI is used on longer cycles. When used with longer cycles, the lag between the cycle peak and crossing the 70 percent mark can be viewed as insurance against being whipsawed.

The RSI has some distinctive characteristics when the estimated cycle length used in the calculation is different from the real cycle length. The perfect 20-day cycle data are used to illustrate these characteristics. Suppose you estimate the cycle to be 50 percent longer than it really is, for example 30 days instead of the correct value of 20 days. Then, you would average the closes up and closes down over a period of 15 days. The upswing part of the RSI would then contain 5 closes down as well as all of the closes up. The addition of the closes down in the denominator of the RSI equation reduces the peak value to less than unity. In much the same way, the downswing part of the RSI contains 5 closes up as well as all the closes down, so the RSI value cannot reach zero. The RSI for a 50-percent-too-long estimate of the cycle period is shown in Figure 6–2. In addition to having reduced amplitude, the peaks of the RSI are delayed relative to the price peaks and its shape is distinctly more triangular. This is due to more smoothing by the longer moving-average period. In such a case with real world data the RSI will be noticeably smoother than the generating price function, RSI will not swing fully between zero and one, and the RSI peaks will lag the price peaks.

A too-short estimate of the cycle length also yields some distinctive RSI patterns. In this case, all the closes are closes up early in the move from the cycle valley toward the cycle peak. Further, all the closes continue to be closes up until the price peak is reached. The result is that the RSI is stuck at a value of

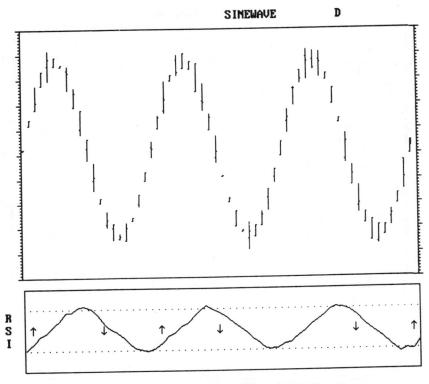

Figure 6–2 RSI Cycle Length Estimated 50% Too Long

one, or "saturated," for a period during the upmove. A similar action occurs on the next half of the cycle. In this case, all the closes are closes down soon after the price passes its peak. All closes continue to be closes down until the price valley is reached. Now, the result is that the RSI is saturated at a value of zero. Figure 6–3 shows the resulting RSI pattern when the true cycle length is underestimated by 50 percent.

The shape and character of the RSI provide clues regarding the goodness of RSI optimization when the market is in the cycle mode. If the RSI repeatedly fails to exceed the 30 percent and 70 percent points, then the length of the estimated cycle is too long. If the RSI is saturated near one and zero, then the

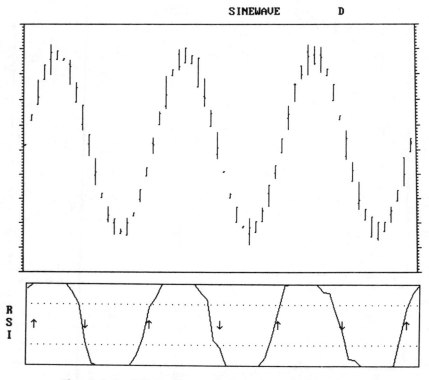

Figure 6–3   RSI Cycle Length Estimated 50% Too Short

estimated cycle length is too short. In general, it is better to make your estimate of the dominant cycle too long rather than too short. The reason for this is that the longer period tends to smooth the RSI function so that whipsawing is avoided and the entry signals are more reliable.

STOCHASTIC

A *stochastic variable* is a random variable that is a function of time. This definition has absolutely nothing to do with a technical trading indicator. The indicator was first developed in the

1960's by Investment Educators. Then, in the early days of computerized technical trading, a group of traders who were to become CompuTrac were sharing ideas. Rick Redmont gave Tim Slater some notes about a new indicator. Tim liked the indicator titled "stochastic process" in those notes. To make a long story short, the name stuck, and this indicator has been popularized by Dr. George Lane.

The definition of the stochastic is mathematically similar to the definition of the RSI, resulting in a normalized function that swings between zero and one. The stochastic compares the current closing price to the "recent" highest high and the lowest low. "Recent" refers to a period selected by the trader. The definition of the stochastic is

$$K = (CL(D) - L)/(H - L)$$

where $CL(D)$ = the current (today's) closing price
H = the highest high price in the selected interval
L = the lowest low price in the selected interval.

Thus a *5-day stochastic* means we compare the current closing price to the highest high price and the lowest low price in the past 5 days.

The stochastic can theoretically swing between zero and one. If the current closing price is equal to the highest high, $K = 1$. It cannot be any larger because the numerator of the definition is equal to the denominator. At the other extreme, if the current closing price is equal to the lowest low, the numerator is zero and therefore the stochastic is zero.

Williams's %R is virtually identical to the stochastic, swinging between one and zero as the stochastic swings between zero and one. Williams's %R is found by subtracting the stochastic from one as

$$\%R = 1 - K$$

$$= (H - CL(D))/(H - L)$$

The close similarity between the definition of %R and the stochastic means that when we optimize one for the dominant cycle, the other is also simultaneously optimized. It is not necessary to distinguish between the two.

In the case of pure sine wave, we always find the highest high and the lowest low within a half cycle of the total wavelength at the time the price is at a turning point. A longer observation period only adds redundant information. However, if the observation period is shorter than a half wavelength we have the chance of either underestimating the highest high when the last close is at a price valley or overestimating the lowest low the last close is at a price peak because we don't reach the true extremes. These situations correspond to those seen in the RSI examples.

With reference to Figure 6–4, the stochastic observation period is a quarter cycle long. At point A, the starting point of the sine function, the current "close" corresponds to the highest high within the observation period, causing the stochastic to have a value of one. The stochastic continues to have a value of (almost) one as time progresses until point B, the peak of the sine wave, is reached. Immediately after point B, the current close is less than the highest high in the observation window, and the stochastic decreases in value. The stochastic (almost) reaches zero when time reaches point C because the current value is also the lowest low during the observation period. The zero value persists until time reaches point D, the price valley. Thereafter, between point D and the next point A, the stochastic rises to its maximum value again, and the cycle repeats. The plot of the stochastic below the sine wave price shows that a too-short estimate results in a saturated stochastic similar to a saturated RSI.

From the cycle perspective, there is no problem in choosing a too-long observation period for the stochastic because the extra data is purely redundant. Therefore, the stochastic is insensitive to an overestimation of cycle length in a sideways

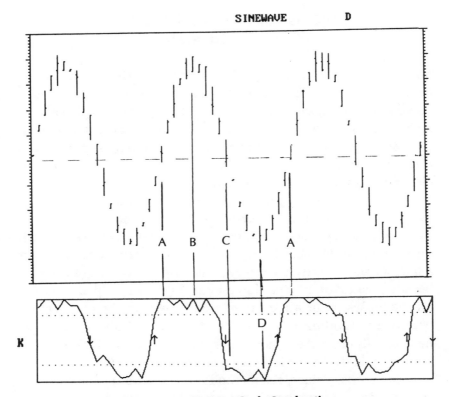

Figure 6–4 Quarter Cycle Stochastic

market. A trending market can consist of the superposition of the cycle on the trendline. In this case, a too-long estimate of the cycle period can distort the highest high or the lowest low so that they are no longer related to the cycle. In these cases when the effects of the trend swamp the cyclic effects, the current close can never swing down to the lowest low in uptrends nor can the current close swing up to the highest high in down-trends. Thus, the result of choosing a too-long stochastic observation period in trending markets is that it is biased near unity in uptrends and biased near zero in downtrends. The short deviations from the bias can result in many false entry signals.

USING RSI AND STOCHASTIC
TO READ THE MARKET

You can use a comparison of the RSI and the stochastic to assess the market condition and to optimize your indicator parameters. Both swing as normalized sine waves in phase with a sine wave generating function. Both become saturated when a too-short estimate of the dominant cycle is made. However, the difference between their characteristics when the estimated cycle length is too long can be exploited.

If the estimated cycle length is too long and the market is in a sideways move, the overestimation will have no effect on the stochastic because the extra data beyond a half wavelength are redundant. On the other hand, a length estimate longer than a half wavelength decreases the peak-to-peak swings of the RSI because the extra information makes the RSI less likely to have all the closes up or all the closes down within the observation period. In trending markets the stochastic tends to be stuck near one limit or the other while the RSI tends to be desensitized and doesn't vary too far from its central value.

Using these clues, the methodology to read the market is to observe RSI and stochastic concurrently, varying the observation period. When the period is less than a half cycle, both will look similar as saturated square waves. Near the half-cycle length both will look sinusoidal. However, as the observation length continues to be increased, the RSI is desensitized and changes its appearance relative to the stochastic. When this occurs, you know too much smoothing is being used and your indicator signals are bound to be too slow.

MOVING AVERAGE
CONVERGENCE/DIVERGENCE (MACD)

MACD was invented by Gerry Appel[2] for the stock market because he noted significant market cycles of 12 to 13 weeks and

24 to 28 weeks. Although developed for weekly markets, MACD has been used with the constants unchanged for daily commodity markets! This must be a truly robust indicator since there is no guarantee that there are 13- or 26-day cycles in commodities.

A *divergence* occurs when the line drawn between successive significant highs of the indicator have a slope opposite that of the line drawn between significant highs of the price. Divergence can also occur between the lines drawn between the significant lows of the indicator and the price. *Convergence* occurs when these lines have the same slope, allowing the indicator to reinforce the direction of the price move. I must confess a personal trading weakness. I cannot see convergences and divergences as they develop in real time. When concentrating on trading and trying to estimate what the future will bring, I cannot define to my own satisfaction what constitutes a significant high (or low). Of course, the definition of a significant high is very clear and the convergence or divergence is easy to see in retrospect. Because of this personal weakness, I completely ignore all convergences and divergences in arriving at my trading strategies. I even ignore them in MACD, where they are part of the name.

I was originally attracted to MACD in much the same way I was attracted to RSI. The time constants were rigidly defined, with no apparent adaptation to current market conditions. Cycle theory can also be applied to MACD to improve its efficacy and, in fact, to provide leading signals for cyclic turns.

The traditional MACD starts with a 13-day exponential moving average (EMA), whose smoothing constant is $2/13 = .15$ (see Chapter 4 for the significance of this conversion rule). A 26-day EMA is calculated next using a smoothing constant of .075 ($2/26 = .075$ approximately). The MACD signal is obtained by subtracting the 26-day EMA from the 13-day EMA. The MACD signal is then smoothed by a 10-day EMA (smoothing constant is $2/10 = .2$). Ignoring the convergence/divergence interpretations, trading signals are obtained when the MACD signal crosses its function, delayed by EMA smoothing. Before we apply cyclic variability to MACD, let's examine some character-istics. It is probably significant that the second EMA is exactly twice the length of the first EMA. There is no special reason to use a 10-day smoothing EMA, so why not smooth with a similar 13-day EMA? Having the third EMA equal to the first EMA is easier to remember, and there is continuity rationale for use with leading indicators.

LEADING INDICATORS

An optimum predictive filter can be derived for a message source having a Poisson probability distribution for its waveform.[3] (A Poisson distribution describes the probability of zero crossings within a given interval for a waveform having a zero mean and swinging between positive and negative values.) Skipping all the heavy math and applying the optimum predictive filter to trad-ing, this filter turns out to be basically the price less its EMA if the price function is modified to have a zero mean. It's surprising that such a simple relationship can have predictive capabilities, but this relationship is fruitful when applied to MACD because MACD comprises a combination of EMAs.

Dealing with the nonlinear phase lag of EMAs can be a little complicated, so the idea of creating leading indicators us-ing simple moving averages (SMA) can perhaps be more easily understood. This is because SMAs have a linear phase relation-ship as a function of the averaging period. From Chapter 4 you recall that the amplitude transfer response of an SMA is $\sin(X)/X$. When the period is a half cycle, X is Pi/2. The result is that the half-cycle SMA lags the sine wave price by Pi/2, or 90 degrees in phase, and is $2/Pi = .637$ of its amplitude. Because $X = Pi/4$ for the quarter-cycle SMA, its phase delay is 45 de-grees and its amplitude is .900. The phasors for the original sine wave price at the dominant cycle and the half-cycle and quarter-cycle SMAs are shown in Figure 6–5a. We perform the vector subtraction of the half-cycle SMA from the quarter-cycle SMA

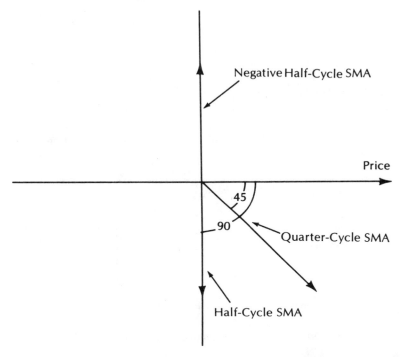

Figure 6–5a   Phasor Diagram for the Quarter-Cycle and Half-Cycle SMAs

by reversing its direction and then doing a vector addition. The results of the vector subtraction of the two SMAs are shown in Figure 6–5b.

The amazing conclusion is that the difference of the quarter-cycle SMA and the half-cycle SMA at the dominant cycle is another sine wave almost exactly in phase with the original sine wave price function! Of course, this result does not occur at all frequencies. When the frequency is very low, both SMAs have very little attenuation and phase shift. Therefore, the difference between the two SMAs is almost zero. The result is that the price is detrended by the SMA difference because the trend can be viewed as a very low-frequency cycle component. At higher frequencies, the SMAs are larger fractions of the wavelength and both moving average components

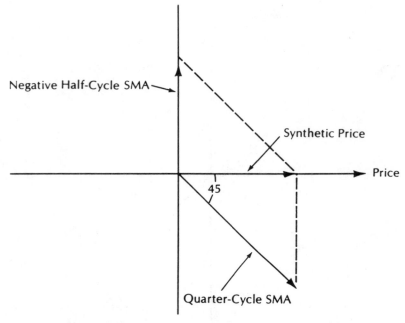

Figure 6–5b   SMA Phasor Construction of Synthetic Price

are attenuated. (We actually prefer EMAs because at these higher frequencies the phase shift cannot exceed 90 degrees so the two components can never add vectorially. Further, the amplitude functions are smooth so that there is always an amplitude difference.) Since the low-frequency trend is removed, since the in-phase dominant cycle exists, and since the high-frequency components are attenuated by the moving average filters, I like to think of the difference of the two moving averages as a *detrended synthetic price.*

The detrended synthetic price result is even more surprising when we reflect that the in-phase difference is generated from two functions that both lagged the original sine wave price. Recognizing this, and recalling the structure of the optimum predictive filter, if we take a quarter-cycle SMA of the detrended synthetic price and subtract this SMA from the synthetic price as in the phasor diagram of Figure 6–6, we see that the resulting

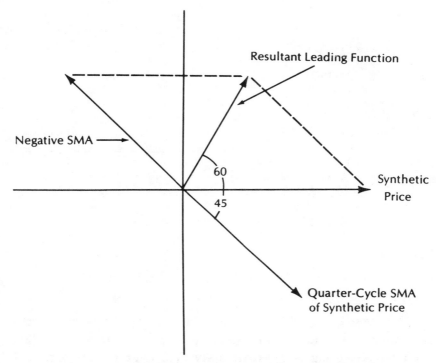

Figure 6–6   SMA Phasor Construction of a Leading Function

function leads the synthetic price (and hence the original price) by approximately 60 degrees. The relationship of the synthetic price and the leading function in the time domain is shown in Figure 6–7.

Figure 6–7 suggests a trading methodology using the leading indicator. When the indicator crosses the synthetic price from the top, sell on the next period because that period will occur very near the cycle peak. Conversely, buy when the indicator crosses the synthetic price from the bottom. I have immodestly dubbed this indicator the ELI, as an acronym for the *Ehlers Leading Indicator.* ELI is clearly a specialized formulation of the MACD momentum based on the optimum predictive filter. But being related to both MACD and the optimum predictive filter, ELI is best formulated using EMAs rather than SMAs.

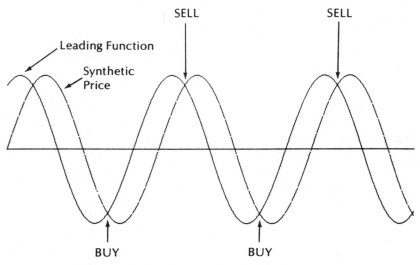

Figure 6–7   Leading Function in the Time Domain

Instead of a half-cycle SMA, we use an EMA whose smoothing function is 3/(*dominant cycle*). Its amplitude response is .436, and its phase lag is approximately 60.5 degrees. Instead of a quarter-cycle SMA we use an EMA whose smoothing function is twice the value of the first EMA. The amplitude response of this second EMA is .702 and its phase lag is approximately 43 degrees. Figure 6–8a shows the phasor differencing of these two EMAs to obtain the detrended synthetic price. It turns out that the phase of the *detrended synthetic price* lags the dominant cycle price function by approximately 17 degrees. We could be closer to the desired zero phase lag, but the EMA smoothing constants would be harder to remember, and any improvement would be negligible (1 day of a 10-day cycle corresponds to 36 degrees). Figure 6–8b shows the phasor differencing of the synthetic price and its EMA using the value of the second smoothing function. In this case, ELI leads the synthetic price by about 44.5 degrees. The ELI amplitude is .682 times the amplitude of the synthetic price. It is desirable to have the ELI and synthetic price have the same amplitude for data being at the dominant cycle. (Other frequency

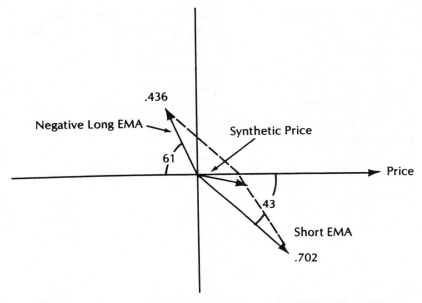

Figure 6–8a   Phasor Construction of the Detrended Synthetic Price

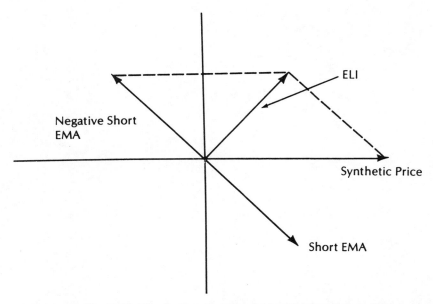

Figure 6–8b   EMA Phasor Construction of Synthetic Price and ELI

components will have varying amplitudes because of differential filter attenuation.) All we need do is to divide ELI by .682 to produce this amplitude normalization.

When we use the MACD as it relates to cycles, we trade simply on the crossing of the ELI and the detrended synthetic price. All convergences and divergences are ignored. My experience is that this is a very robust trading system when the market is in the cyclic mode.

7

SETTING STOPS

Technical trading seems to put extreme emphasis on finding the right entry point for a trade, and scant attention is paid to techniques to exit a trade. There are times when it would not be hard to convince me that a trade can be entered almost anywhere and overall profitability would really be established by the way the trades were exited. The purpose of this chapter is to establish a logical and coherent method of stop-loss placement using cycle information.

KEY STOP ELEMENTS

An effective stop-loss system must allow sufficient risk to give the trade a chance to "breathe." The system also must include features that minimize loss of profit after the expected movement has occurred. Using these criteria, the key elements of the stop system are setting the initial value of the stop and then using a method to accelerate, or tighten, the stop as time progresses.

THE INITIAL STOP-LOSS PLACEMENT

The average value of price can have a measurable short-term cycle. These cycles can have a high-frequency price action that can be treated as superimposed noise unrelated to the cycle. For example, the intraday activity can be considered "noise" on a daily bar chart. If we want to allow enough risk for our trade to breathe and accommodate the noise variations, we must set the stop-loss so the noise will not erroneously take us out of a desirable trade. The obvious solution is to use the average daily trading range, or volatility, as a key to setting the stop on a daily basis.

Using daily volatility is a logical method of setting the initial stop-loss so the stop-loss adapts to the current market conditions. Daily volatility is just the difference between the high and low price for the day. Averaging the daily volatility over the last half cycle of prices provides a reasonable measure of the current noise level. This average volatility is subtracted from the low price of the day of entry (for a long position) to establish the stop for the next day's trading. Of course, the average volatility is added to the entry day's high price to place the stop for a short position.

Using this system, an entry is made at the opening price based on the ELI leading indicator or by stop-and-reverse (SAR) from a previous stop-loss value. There is no stop placed on the day of entry. This is because there is no clear-cut way to establish this stop. For example, entry into the position could occur from a previous stop-and-reverse strategy. In such a system the stop may not be touched, and it is not possible to place a stop on a position you have not already established. In many cases you don't even know in a timely manner if your stop has been touched. The average volatility almost requires a limit move to trigger the initial stop in many cases, and no stop can protect against a limit move.

In any event, the first key element of stop-loss placement is that the initial stop is placed a distance equal to the average daily trading range below the low (or above the high) of the day of entry. The average is taken over a period equal to half the dominant cycle.

ACCELERATION

The purpose of introducing an acceleration factor into stop placement is to successively tighten the stop to preserve accumulated profits when the price makes a significant reversal. We can use the dominant cycle to establish the criteria for a significant reversal. If we know the length of the short-term price cycle, we know the optimum duration of the trade is half the cycle period. The best long position phase of the half cycle takes us from the valley of the price to its peak. The best short position phase takes us from the peak to the valley. Knowing this, we will derive the acceleration term so that a trade reversal occurs every half cycle of a theoretical pure sine wave price.

The stop-loss strategy is to remove a fraction of the difference between the previous day's low price and its stop value (for a long position). This fraction increases linearly as the age of the trade increases so that by the time the trade age reaches the period of the half cycle, the entire difference is removed to set the stop for the next day. This accelerating stop strategy allows the trade to mature gracefully. Very little difference between the day's low price and its stop is removed in setting the stop for the next day's trading early in the trade. Nonetheless, profits are protected because the next day's stop is raised if today's low is higher than before. When the age of the trade reaches the length of half the dominant cycle, removing the entire difference means the price would have to increase dramatically to avoid touching the stop on the next day.

The equation for setting the long position stop for the next trading period is

$$\text{Stop}\,(D + 1) = \text{Low}\,(D) - (1 - 2 * \text{Age}/DC) * (\text{Low}\,(D) - \text{Stop}\,(D))$$

where D = Today
$D + 1$ = Tomorrow
DC = Dominant cycle length (in days).

When the age of the trade is zero at the entry of the trade, the equation reduces to

$$\text{Stop}\,(D+1) = \text{Low}\,(D) - (\text{Low}\,(D) - \text{Stop}\,(D))$$

$$= \text{Stop}\,(D)$$

In this case, the next stop is equal to the previous stop. By the time the age of the trade reaches half the dominant cycle length, the term $(1 - 2 * \text{Age}/DC)$ reduces to zero so that the next stop is exactly the current low price. As the age of the trade exceeds half the dominant cycle, the $(1 - 2 * \text{Age}/DC)$ term becomes negative, canceling the negative sign preceding it. The current stop must always be below the current low price, otherwise the trade would be stopped out. Thus, for the case of the age exceeding the half dominant cycle length, the next stop will be higher than the previous low price. The price must accelerate rapidly to avoid being stopped out for longer and longer trade ages.

The basic idea of the accelerating stop can be seen with reference to Figure 7–1, where the solid line is the history of the

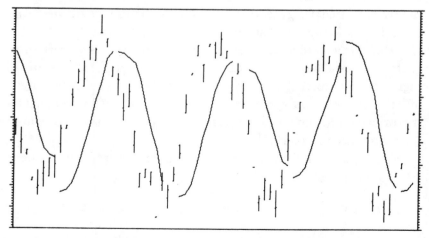

Figure 7–1　Stop Acceleration Optinially Set for Sinewave Price in Noise

stop values relative to a sine wave price with superimposed noise. If we overestimate the cycle length, the stop does not accelerate as fast, and the cyclic price tends to collapse back toward the stop before the trade exited. The effects of a too-long estimate of the dominant cycle is shown in Figure 7–2. Although some profit is sacrificed, the system is still workable. On the other hand, if the estimated cycle length is too short, the stop accelerates very rapidly, intersecting the price while the price is still making its move. Figure 7–3 shows how the too-short estimate of cycle length can introduce whipsaw trades. These whipsaw trades must be avoided because they can consume profit in a hurry. In general, it is preferable to make a too-long estimate of the dominant cycle rather than a too-short estimate when using this stop strategy.

The basic idea of the stop system can be modified several ways to produce enhanced performance. For example, the $(1 - 2 * \text{Age}/DC)$ term can be changed to $(1 - \text{Age}/(K * DC))$. K can be some number larger than 0.5, for example, 0.7. If K is 0.7 and you input the true dominant cycle, then the entire gap

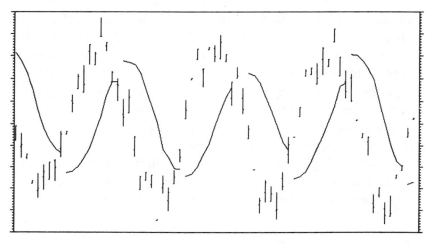

Figure 7–2 Overestimation of Cycle Length Slows Acceleration, Reducing Profit (Stop-Loss Is Solid Line)

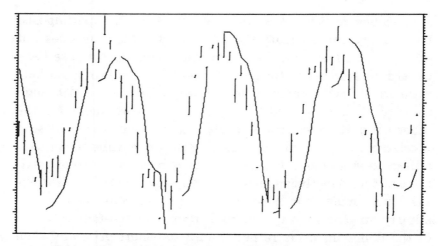

Figure 7–3 Underestimated Cycle Length Speeds Stop Acceleration— Resulting Whipsaws Severely Reduce Profits (Stop-Loss Is Solid Line)

between the current low price and the current stop will not be removed until the age of the trade is 70% of the dominant cycle. This variation ensures that you will err on the long side of your cycle input to compute the stops, resulting in fewer whipsaw reversals. You can also make the $Age/(K * DC)$ term nonlinear by multiplying it by itself one or more times, with the result that the term is square, cubed, and so forth. When you do this, the factor becomes much smaller when the ratio is less than one and much larger when the ratio is greater than one, thereby making it more nonlinear. Another variant on the stop system is to multiply the measured average daily volatility by a constant to either decrease or increase the initial risk. Providing flexibility in setting the risk can alter the overall profits of the system.

I have a high regard for this stop-loss system. This stop system, combined with the ELI indicator described in Chapter 6, are the heart of the EPOCH PRO trading program.

8

CYCLE MEASUREMENT

Cycles in the market can be measured in a variety of ways that involve a range of complexity, with resulting accuracy differences. In this chapter we discuss the most commonly used approaches. The most commonly used measurement techniques are cycle finders, Fast Fourier Transforms (FFT), and Maximum Entropy Spectral Analysis (MESA).

I *do not* think FFTs are appropriate for the measurement of short-term market cycles. The practical application of FFTs leaves much to be desired because some of the fundamental constraints are ignored when looking at the market. Cycle finders are nice for historical research, but if cycles are apparent in real-time trading their existence will be obvious to many traders. If the majority of traders establish positions on the basis of the cycle, the cycle is extinguished. As an example, seasonals are most often discounted at the time the contract begins trading.

CYCLE FINDERS

The basic idea of cycle finders is to measure the distance between the same phase on successive cycles. The resultant measurement is necessarily the cycle length of a simple cycle. Any constant phase point on the cycle can be used, but the measurement is usually made between cycle lows. Cycle lows are used not only because they are easy to identify but because they tend to be sharper than cycle highs.

A cycle finder can be as simple as a ruler or dividers that measure lengths on printed charts. The *Ehrlich Cycle Finder*[1] named after inventor Stan Ehrlich, is basically a pantograph that allows you mechanically to correlate successive cycles and to scale cycle periods in the search for more complicated patterns.

Cycle finders are also found on most Toolbox trading programs such as CompuTrac, N-Squared Computing, and MetaStock. Typical operation involves placing the screen cursor at a critical time position of interest. When the cycle finder tool is called, a vertical line is drawn at the cursor position and other vertical lines are repeated every cycle period to the right and left of the critical position. The up-arrow and down-arrow keys typically adjust the cycle length, the length being the spacing between vertical lines. The left-arrow and right-arrow keys typically control the time position of all the lines by moving them together.

Cycle finders are handy devices for a quick inspection of cyclic activity and estimation of the next cyclic turn of the market. What the cycle finders have in speed and simplicity is compromised by their inability to address all but the most obvious cases.

FAST FOURIER TRANSFORMS (FFT)

A *Fourier transform* is a procedure to find the frequency response of a function whose time domain characteristic is known.

As it relates to the market, a Fourier transform measures the cycles from the bar chart where time is the horizontal axis and the price is scaled along the vertical axis. The transform produces a spectragram (see Figure 8–1) where the cycle amplitudes are displayed as a function of frequency. Engineers and scientists usually prefer the transform to be displayed in terms of frequency rather than period (cycle length). A *fast Fourier transform* (FFT) is an algorithm used to speed the calculation because a large number of mathematical operations are required in taking the transform. The FFT has particular application when the length of the data are long.

Fourier transforms are the equivalent of applying the time data to a bank of filters. Energy input to this bank of filters can have components at all frequencies. Conceptually, one of these filters could be tuned to output energy only for a 6-day cycle and

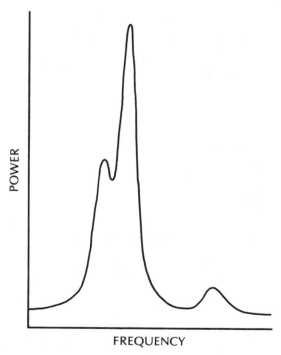

Figure 8–1   Spectragram of a Complex Signal

rejecting all other energy. Another filter could be tuned to 7 days, a third filter could be tuned to 8 days, and so forth. Then the frequency response of the complex input data is computed by comparing the amplitude of the energy at the output of each of the filters in the bank. If we stacked the filters from left to right so that the X-axis is the cycle frequency and plotted the output energy of each filter parallel to the Y-axis, the result would be a discrete spectrum in terms of the cycle frequency. By simple examination of the spectrum we could see which filter has the strongest output and therefore what is the dominant cycle in the data. We could also easily spot secondary cycles of lower amplitude if they were present.

Fourier transforms do this filtering mathematically. If the input data is multiplied by a sine wave and the product of all the discrete points are added over exactly a complete cycle, only energy at the frequency of the sine wave results. The energy is additive over multiple complete cycles. If the input data is also multiplied by a cosine wave and the product of all the discrete points are added, another energy term is obtained only for the frequency of the cosine wave. Adding the two energy terms together recovers the entire energy in the input data at the frequency of the sine wave. That is, we have mathematically accomplished the equivalent of filtering.

A very important constraint in the Fourier transform is that the data must be taken only over an integer number of cycles.

When taking a Fourier transform, the user obtains a sample of data to satisfy the integer number of cycle constraint. In theory, this sample of data is perfectly representative of all data extending in both directions to infinity. That is, data in the window is replicated over and over again in the complete picture.

A final constraint of the sampled data system is the *Nyquist sampling criterion.* The Nyquist criterion states that the shortest cycle must have at least two samples per cycle. Therefore, the shortest cycle that can be measured using daily data is a 2-day cycle.

Let's see where these constraints lead us if we analyze the market with a 64-sample FFT. Each sample can be a day's data, so we are using about 13 weeks of data on a daily basis. The longest cycle that fits in this sample window is 64 days. The next longest cycle fitting an integer number of times is a 32-day cycle. The next longest cycle is 64/3, or 21.3 days. The fourth longest cycle is 64/4, or 16 days. Note there is a gap, or lack of resolution of more than 5 days just in the region we wish to examine for trading short-term cycles. We have a dilemma. We cannot measure an 18-day cycle and still have the Fourier transform be valid. The only way to increase the resolution is to increase the size of the data window. Suppose we increased the data window to 256 samples (days). Now there are 14 cycles of a signal whose period is 18.29 days and 15 cycles of a signal whose period is 17.07 days. We have achieved an approximate 1-day resolution with the 256 data samples, but the penalty is severe.

The only way we can get the FFT resolution we need is to use more than one year's data. The short-term 18-day cycle can only be identified if it has been occurring consistently for the last 14 or 15 cycles! If we accept the drunkard's walk formulation as the basis for chart activity, the data-length requirement is unacceptable. The requirement is similar to demanding that 14 river meanders in a row all be identical to predict the occurrence of the next meander. This is so unlikely that the possibility should be dismissed out of hand.

FFTs lack resolution when the data window is short. Longer data bases force an unlikely requirement on continued existence of the cycle. For these reasons we should reject FFTs for the identification of short-term cycles in the market.

MAXIMUM ENTROPY SPECTRAL ANALYSIS (MESA)

MESA is an outgrowth of the predictive deconvolution filtering techniques developed by geophysicists for oil exploration.[2,3] Its specific goal is to obtain high resolution measurements from minimum length data—precisely the requirement for the identification of short-term cycles in the market.

If we have a frequency source followed by a filter, the output of the filter is just those frequency components of the filter that were allowed to pass through the filter. This is mathematically expressed as the product of the frequency source and the filter in the frequency domain. We can find the Fourier series (not to be confused with the Fourier transform) for both the source and the filter to obtain a description in the time domain. The process of taking the product of the two Fourier series is called *convolution*. Convolution is the equivalent of sliding the filter time response past the source time response, taking the product at each time increment, and summing all the products.

The *maximum entropy* approach to spectral analysis is a variation of deconvolution filtering techniques. A deconvolution filter whitens the spectrum of the signal on which it operates; that is, when convolved with the original signal it outputs a new signal with a constant spectrum. A constant spectrum signal is called white noise because it contains energy at all frequencies. This approach to spectral analysis is also known as the Markov spectrum or the autoregressive spectrum. Burg realized that this approach yields the spectrum having the "maximum entropy" of all possible spectra that are consistent with the measured autocorrelation function. *Entropy* is a term first used in thermodynamics to describe the degree of disorder and has more recently been used as a quantitative term in information theory. Therefore, "maximum entropy" is a case having the least amount of information, and deconvolution filtering produces an output having the least amount of information.

The advantage of deconvolution filtering is immediately obvious. Finding the frequency spectrum does not involve a convolution in the frequency domain with a cumbersome window spectrum (the FFT period) that unavoidably destroys spectral resolution. The convolution has already taken place in the time domain between the input signal and the digital filter. Therefore, no window sidelobes or serious end effects exist with the FFT. The truncation of the data set is important only to the extent that enough data must be available to allow the building of an efficient whitening filter that can reduce the output data to a random series. This is routinely done using only about one cycle's worth of input data.

The maximum entropy estimate is the optimal choice for measuring cycles because it is maximally noncommittal with regard to any missing data and is simultaneously constrained to be consistent with all available data. The "correct" length of data to be used for analysis is perhaps the most critical aspect of using MESA. In any event, the fact that MESA attains its high-resolution measurement with a short amount of data makes its use ideal for the market where current measurements are mandatory for relevant results.

9

How MESA Works

There is an easier way to understand how MESA works by relating its operation to the circuit diagram of Figure 9–1. Instead of putting a signal into the filter and getting white noise out, as we described in the previous chapter, we turn the process around. That is, we start with a white noise source (containing all frequencies at uniform amplitudes) and apply it to a tunable filter. By turning the problem around, we expect to see a time domain signal at the output of the filter. We take this filter output and compare it with the real time domain data we input into the program. The comparison is done in the comparitor circuit. The output of the comparitor is used to tune the filter. Filter tuning continues until the output of the comparitor is as close to zero as we can get in the RMS (Root Mean Square) sense. That is, the filter is tuned to be maximally consistent with the input data.

When the filter is tuned we have a replica of the data we input. However, there is now a major difference. We have described the data in terms of the transfer response of the filter. In other words, we have created an accurate model of the data.

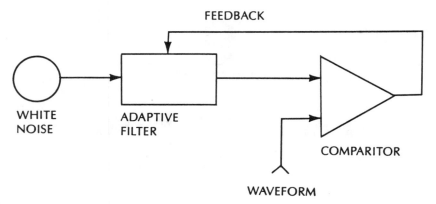

Figure 9–1   How the MESA Filter Is Tuned

The filter transfer response can be described as a rational fraction of two polynomials as

$$F(x) = \frac{a_0 + a_1 x + a_2 x^2 + a_3 x^3 + \ldots}{b_0 + b_1 x + b_2 x^2 + b_3 x^3 + \ldots}$$

According to the fundamental theorem of algebra, we can factor the polynomials in both the numerator and denominator so the transfer response can be written as:

$$F(x) = \frac{(x - z_1) * (x - z_2) * (x - z_3) * \ldots}{(x - p_1) * (x - p_2) * (x - p_3) * \ldots}$$

Written this way, we can see precisely those values of x where the transfer response goes to zero. These values occur at z_1, z_2, z_3, and so forth. These z's are called the zeros of the transfer response. Similarly, we can tell the denominator goes to zero when $x = p_1$, $x = p_2$, and so forth. The transfer response goes to infinity at these points because the denominator goes to zero. These points are called the poles of the transfer function.

Picture the response as the elevation of a circus tent. The two horizontal dimensions of the tent are analogous to the "complex" plane of the frequency response. The complex plane consists of the "real" and "imaginary" dimensions. There are points on the tent where the tent is staked to the ground. These are the zeros. There are other points where the poles are inserted to produce the high peaks. The use of poles to describe the zero denominator positions is obvious. The frequency response of the filter is similar to the path a marble would take if we released it to roll on the surface of the tent. The marble is constrained to roll only in a straight line along the real frequency. For reasons of conservation of energy, poles cannot occur at real frequencies. Otherwise, we would get more energy out of the filter than we put in.

The generalized filter can have several forms. We could use the numerator only, the denominator only, or both the numerator and denominator in the model.

If the filter uses only the numerator, the model is called a *moving average* (MA) model. We can create an MA model by fitting a polynomial to the price data.[1] Because this procedure is curve fitting in the purest sense, MA models are not recommended. There is no validity for projections made outside the bounds defining the curve because there is no principle, like cycles, to assert that the curve should continue.

Van Den Bos[2] has shown that the MESA filter is equivalent to the least-squares fitting of the discrete-time all-pole model to the data. In other words, MESA only uses the denominator as its filter. MESA is an *autoregressive* (AR) model. The replica signal at the output of the filter is curve fitted to the real price data. However, this replica is only used as a means to tune the filter so the spectral content can be estimated. The filter is the cyclic model of the market, and the telegrapher's equation tells us we can expect coherent behavior when the market is in the cycle mode. That is, the MESA model has a short-term predictive capability.

ARIMA is both a *moving average* (MA) and *autoregressive* (AR) model, using the numerator and denominator of the filter model transfer response. While more theoretically general, it is not preferred to MESA because of its tendency to produce spurious filter responses. These spurious responses occur when the filter is overspecified in terms of the order of the polynomials. When overspecified, the filter attempts to reduce to the order of the filter by providing a zero to cancel a pole. If the cancellation is not exact, the misalignment of the stake and the pole in the tent surface can cause the marble to roll much differently than if neither existed. Since there is no real way to determine the correct order of the filter, ARIMA models have a tendency toward spurious responses when the order of the filter is kept high to obtain the desired frequency resolution.

Of the three kinds of models that can be formed from the rational filter transfer response, MESA is preferred because it has the least tendency toward spurious responses and because it has a short-term predictive capability. Scientific research is continuing to improve the spectral estimate in the presence of noise.

DATA LENGTH

The most critical decision to be made using MESA is the length of data to be used for the analysis. One of the major applications of a filter is to eliminate the noise in order to clarify the action of the cyclic signal. Early versions of MESA maximized the output *signal-to-noise* ratio to establish the "correct" length of data to be used for analysis. On a given day the analysis was repeated using different data lengths, and the data length that produced the highest signal-to-noise ratio was finally used as the output.

The cycle measurement made using this criteria was basically a "snapshot" for the given day. The cycle measurement made on the next day was a completely independent snapshot. While fine in theory, this approach led to difficulties in interpretation. Basically, the trader tried to string the snapshots together to make a "movie" under the assumption that the cycle activity does not change dramatically from day to day. Unfortunately, the independent measurements produced a "movie" that was so jerky that interpretation of cycle activity was difficult.

Interpretation of the market cyclic activity was improved by changing the criterion for the length of data to use for analysis. The new criterion emphasizes continuity. Knowing that MESA requires only about one cycle's worth of data to make a measurement, the data length used for "today's" measurement is "yesterday's" cycle length. This algorithm tends to preclude the preference for a longer cycle when MESA has already focused on a shorter cycle. For example, assume a 10-day cycle is currently in force as the dominant cycle and a 40-day cycle is also present. Using a longer data sample, MESA would probably jump to the 40-day cycle length on the basis of having the maximum signal-to-noise ratio. MESA would select the longer cycle length because the 10-day cycle would have to be present for the entire 40-day span to compete with the 40-day cycle. The 10-day cycle would also confront the principle of proportionality—the 40-day cycle amplitude is probably larger. By using a shorter data length when a shorter cycle has previously been measured, the bias to the longer cycle lengths is removed and MESA has greater inertia, avoiding jerky day-to-day measurements. The continuity resulting from using the previous dominant cycle period as the new data length allows the measurements to move smoothly between short dominant cycles and longer dominant cycles and back as these cycles ebb and flow. Sometimes, when tradable cycles are not present, the cycle length measurement is erratic.

Jerkiness in the cyclic measurement can, in fact, aid interpretation of market activity. Cyclic measurements are most erratic when the market is in a trend mode and there is little useful cyclic activity. Therefore, when the MESA cycle measurements are erratic, you should avoid trading on the basis of cycles. One of the key uses of MESA is to detect when the market is in the cycle mode and when it is in the trend mode. By identification of these modes you know when to shift your trading strategy to fit the current market conditions.

PREDICTIONS

The MESA filter outputs data in the time domain that is a true replica of the real data. The big difference between the real data and the filter is that the filter is a model of the price function and has the ability to produce predictions. The predictions are based on the assumption that the cycles measured in the recent past will continue into the future.

One simple example of a predictor is a crystal goblet an opera singer tries to break with her voice. The opera singer adjusts the pitch of her voice to the resonant frequency of the goblet and the goblet starts to ring. If the singer suddenly stops, the goblet continues to ring and is a predictor of the note the singer would have made. In this simple example the goblet is a single pole filter with only one resonant frequency. Moreover, the singer had to adjust to the filter rather than the filter adjusting to the singer. But the point is that when a filter pole is excited, it continues to ring for a short while just as if the input energy were still present. This ringing is still true even when the filter is complex and has a larger number of poles.

The MESA digital filter has been tuned to all the cycles between 8 and 50 days. By allowing the digital clock to run into the future, a prediction is formed by combining all the measured cycles in their measured amplitudes and phases. The prediction is made by projecting the ringing one day into the future. Then this day is taken to be "real" data so that another prediction can be made one more day forward. The prediction is therefore subject to cumulative error buildup the further the prediction is carried into the future. The prediction is therefore limited to 10 periods to avoid accumulation of large errors.

MESA makes cycle measurements throughout the entire contract. The "fearless forecast" made by the prediction is easy to backtest. Greater confidence can be placed in the timing of the predicted turning points by backtesting the prediction for several days and seeing if the predicted turning point remains stationary. There is no definitive way to measure the accuracy of the prediction because it spans a 10-day period. The definition of accuracy can vary over that period. Here are some examples for which accuracy is sought: How well does MESA call the direction of the next day's trading? How accurately does MESA call the timing of the turning point? How accurately does MESA call the level at which a turn is made?

My answers to these questions are qualitative and are based on using the program over the years. First, MESA works best when the market is in the cycle mode. The cycle mode generally occurs when the market is otherwise described as in a trading range or in a sideways movement. MESA predictions can be used simply to call the direction of the next day's move.[3] MESA predictions can be used as a timing device to anticipate turning points but are just awful in predicting the level at which the turns will be made. These are simply observations, and I have no rationale to justify them. Cycles certainly exist when the market is in the trend mode, but it is generally unwise to take a position against the trend because the slope of the trend can cancel the contraslope of the cycle. On the other hand, the predicted cycle turning point can be used to pick an advantageous entry point for trades in the direction of the trend.

MESA predictions are most valid when the measured cycle has been stable in recent history, a period on the order of a half-cycle length. The longer the stability the better, but short-term cycles seldom remain stable for several cycle lengths. If the recent cycle measurement shows a changing from one cycle length to another, the historical data record contains old cycle information that distorts the prediction from representing the current dominant cycle. Greater confidence can be placed on the prediction of a turning point if that turning point prediction remains consistent over several successive predictions.

10

USING THE SPECTRUM TO IDENTIFY CYCLES AND TRENDS

Examples of responses described by spectrums surround us. Colors we see can be described by their wavelengths. Spectrums help us describe transfer responses as amplitudes of a function of frequency. For example, common glass is used to construct greenhouses because the glass allows the (relatively) long wavelength *infrared* radiation to pass and be absorbed by the plants. On the other hand, you will never get a sunburn in a greenhouse because the glass panels block the shorter wavelength *ultraviolet* radiation.

Spectrum displays are useful to interpret cyclic market activity because the relative amplitude of combinations of cycles can help you sort the information. Your resulting interpretations can help you predict future market activity and improve the quality of the predictions.

SPECTRUM DEFINED

It is more convenient to describe market cycles in terms of their wavelength instead of their frequency. We commonly refer to these wavelengths as "an 18-day cycle," for example. In our description of Fourier transforms in Chapter 8 we described the time/frequency transform as the equivalent of applying the signal to a bank of filters. The combined output of this bank of filters is the *spectrum*. The amplitude at the output of the 6-day filter only has energy at that wavelength; the output of the 7-day filter only has energy at the 7-day wavelength; and so on. Figure 10–1 is a diagram of how the spectrum is created and displayed. The complex time waveform is applied to all of the filters, and each filter only allows its tuned frequency component to pass. An amplitude detector is connected to the output of each filter, so the amplitudes displayed relative to the filter numbers fundamentally comprise a spectrum.

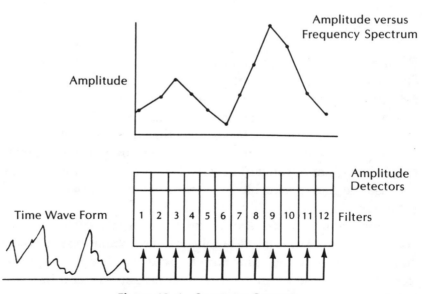

Figure 10–1   Spectrum Concept

The spectrum display is always amplitude of the cycle primitive as a function of frequency (or wavelength) of the total waveform. The spectrum can tell us by inspection whether there is more than one cycle present in the composite waveform. If there are two or more cycle components, the spectrum reveals their relative amplitudes and therefore their relative importance to future market activity, under the assumption that the measured cycles will continue.

The spectrum will appear as a single spike as shown in Figure 10–2 when a single frequency is present in the price. In many cases the frequency resolution is reduced. That is, the spike becomes broader because the cyclic energy is not focused at a single cycle period. Instead, the total cyclic energy is smeared around a central average period, as shown in Figure 10–3. A common way to designate a "good" cyclic spectrum from a "poor"

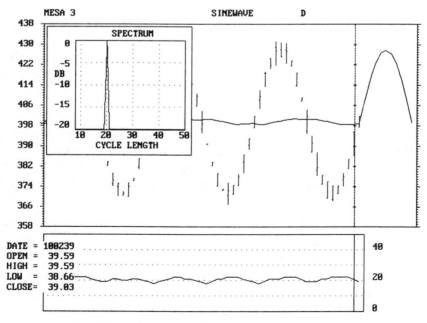

Figure 10–2　Spectrum for Pure 20-Day Sinewave

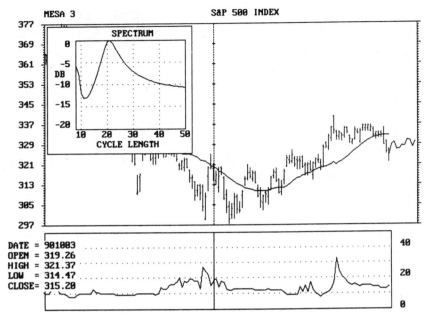

Figure 10–3   Poor Resolution Spectrum

one is by the quality, or *Q* factor. Cyclic *Q* can be defined as the ratio of the center (peak amplitude) wavelength to the width of the spectrum curve at the half power (−3 dB) points. A *Q* factor of 4 or more says that most of the cyclic energy is concentrated near the wavelength having the peak amplitude, and therefore we have a high-quality, high-resolution cyclic condition. Poor resolution results when cyclic energy is spread across a range of frequencies as shown in Figure 10–4. A sharp step in price often results in low-resolution spectrums because a wide range of frequencies is required if we are to synthesize the step from cyclic components. The spectrum simply analyzes the components that really comprise the step function.

Touching on signal synthesis, we generated a rudimentary sawtooth waveform in Chapter 3 by combining a cycle with its second harmonic at half amplitude and its third harmonic at one-third amplitude. Figure 10–5 shows this synthesized waveform in

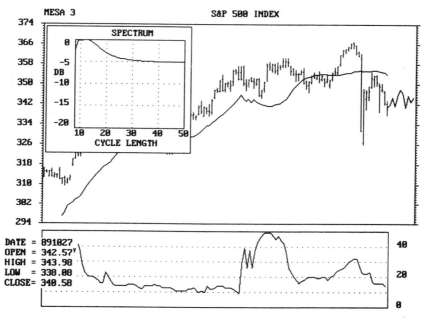

Figure 10–4   Bad Resolution Spectrum

terms of a bar chart. The fundamental frequency is a 42-day cycle. The second harmonic is a 21-day cycle, and the third harmonic is a 14-day cycle. Figure 10–5 also shows the spectrum for this synthesized waveform, as measured by MESA.

TREND ONSET IDENTIFICATION

MESA-measured spectra can be used for early identification of the onset of a trend. We use the principles of superposition and proportionality for this interpretation. The spectrum identifies the frequency components in the price, isolating the components contributing to the trend. Perhaps the best way to describe the identification process is with an example, as shown in Figures 10–6 through 10–9.

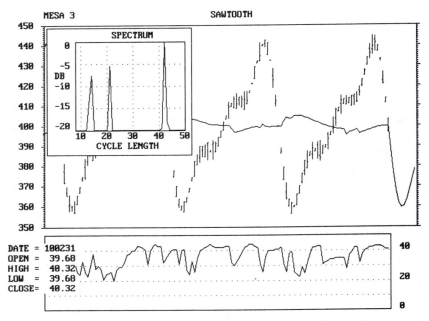

Figure 10–5   Spectrum of Synthesized 42-Day Sawtooth

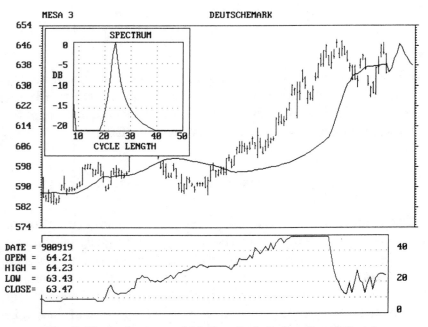

Figure 10–6   Spetrum of 24-Day Cycle Before Trend Onset

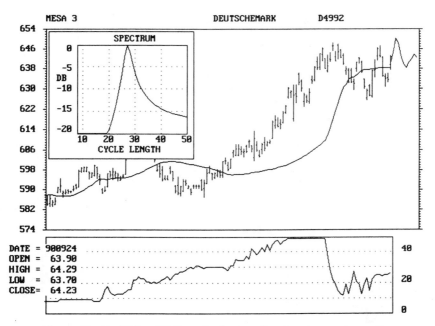

Figure 10–7 Rising 50-Day Cycle Amplitude Warns of Trend

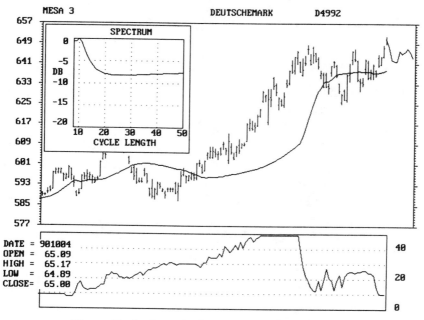

Figure 10–8 Long Cycle Spectrum Shows Trend

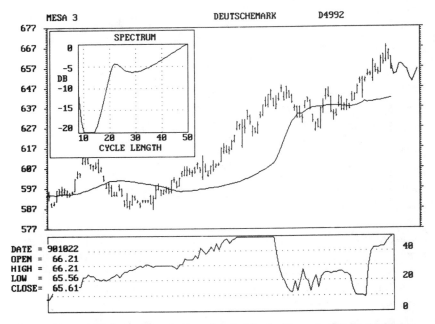

Figure 10–9 High Amplitude Trend Amplitude Swamps Short Cycle Spectrum Amplitudes

Figure 10–6 shows the market having only a single 24-day cyclic component. There is no hint of a trend developing. As time progresses to Figure 10–7, we start to see low level long wavelength components because the "tail" of the spectrum starts to lift off the −20 dB baseline. Time progress still further in Figure 10–8 where the frequency components longer than 50 days clearly identify the trend onset. MESA identifies the trend segment as a piece of a very long cycle. Since the principle of proportionality prevails, that long-term cycle has an amplitude stronger than the short-term cycle within the spectrum window. Finally, with the trend in full force, the trend amplitude swamps the short-term cycle.

Recognizing how the spectrum "tail" lifts off the baseline as a trend develops helps us use such patterns as early warnings of trends. The reading works equally well at the termination of the trend. We can watch the spectrum tail drop down to the baseline day-by-day as the trend is extinguished.

Trend identification is important because now MESA not only can help us trade during cyclic market activity but also can help us set trading strategy—shifting from cycle mode strategy to trend mode strategy and back. Cycle analysis is one of the fastest ways to identify trend characteristics because the onset of the trend results from the failure of a cycle. Cycle failure can be identified within a half cycle of the full period in the time domain, and the unique characteristics of the spectrum display provide clues even sooner. Fast identification of the trend onset and exhaustion allows you to capture a larger percentage of the move without whipsaws.

11

PUTTING IT ALL TOGETHER

Previous chapters have addressed various concepts and theories without particular attention for application to trading. All the theories in the world are of no benefit unless they have a practical application. That's the purpose of this chapter. We will tie the concepts together in a coordinated way to create a trading methodology. In the next chapter we show how this methodology is used in a practical example.

MODELS SUIT MORE THAN CLOTHES

Since the market consists of several distinctive modes such as trends, seasonals, random, and short-term cycles, the first goal is to identify the current market mode. We do this by first creating a simple model of the market. This model consists of a trend plus a dominant cycle. The model is a first-order model because complex combinations of cycles are not considered.

Also, seasonal variations are lumped together with trends, and both are considered the trend for the moment. The simple model also does not directly consider the sideways random market, where additional interpretation is required.

The simple model only has two components—the cycle and the trend. If we know one of these components, we automatically know the other because we know the total market. If we know the dominant cycle, we can obtain the trend simply by subtracting the cyclic component from the total market. Mathematically, if we know two components of an equation we can solve for the third component. That's exactly what MESA does. MESA first accurately measures the cycles in the market and identifies the dominant cycle among all the measured cycles. MESA also takes a simple average equal to the length of the dominant cycle. This average removes the dominant cycle component, as explained in Chapter 4. This average is a point, when plotted on the bar chart, positioned at the day the simple average was taken. This point has been stripped of the dominant cycle component. If we repeat this each day, taking different averages as the dominant cycle changes, we can connect the points to form an "instantaneous trendline." Quotation marks are used for the instantaneous trendline because a trendline is recovered only for the simplistic model. In actual practice the instantaneous trendline contains seasonals, secondary cycles, and other components that are ignored by the model.

Although imperfect, the mathematical model puts the market on display in a way that we traders can understand.

ROLE MODELS SHOW THE WAY

We next examine the price action of the market relative to the instantaneous trendline. When the market is in a cycle mode, the price alternates back and forth across the trendline every half cycle. This alternation was schematically shown in Figures 2–1 and 3–9, for example. This is the fundamental definition of the cycle mode. On the other hand, when the market breaks into a trend the price stays on one side of the trendline. This is the same action a trending market takes with any moving average. The difference is that the instantaneous trendline is a very special kind of moving average. The special characteristic is that the period of the moving average is adapted to the current market conditions. It enables one of the earliest identifications of the onset of a trend.

Trend identification is straightforward. If the price range fails to touch the instantaneous trendline within a half cycle of the measured dominant cycle, a trend is declared to be in force. This is one of the quickest ways to detect the onset of the trend mode because the trend is established by inference from the measured cycle instead of being measured directly. The usual lag accompanying conventional moving averages is avoided. The cycle mode fails because the trend overwhelms the cycle amplitude, holding the price in the direction of the trend. As a result, the price fails to cross the instantaneous trendline. Cycle failure in the time domain can be reinforced with observations regarding the spectrum shape, as we discussed in Chapter 10.

The instantaneous trendline can be curved. This is a natural result of including the seasonals and secondary cycles in the definition of a trend. A typical MESA trendline is shown in Figure 11–1 as the solid line. MESA indicates the concurrent measure dominant cycle, recalculated daily, below the bar chart on the same time scale, with the vertical scale running from zero to 50 days. On any given day, the onset of the trend is determined by counting backward half the number of days, as indicated on the dominant cycle display. The cursor location in Figure 11–1 is at the onset of a trend on 10/23/90. (The date is in the YYMMDD format in the tabular data on the chart). On this date the measured dominant cycle was 14 days as shown on the cycle display. Counting backward, and including the current day, the price has not touched the instantaneous trendline in the past 7 days (half the measured dominant cycle). Therefore, we declare the onset of the trend to have occurred on this date. The trend continues in

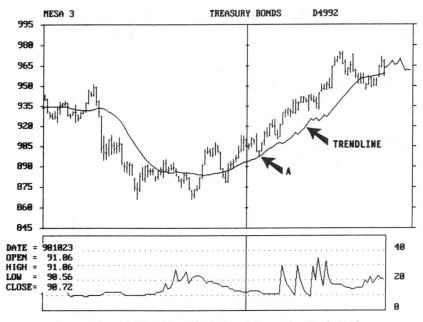

Figure 11-1 MESA Identifies Trend Onset by Cycle Failure

force until the price again touches the trendline. It is possible for the price to dip down and touch the trendline for a day or two, such as at point A, before resuming the trend. In such cases, declaring the trend still to be in force is a judgment call.

The simplified model and the accurate MESA cycle measurement enable you to assess the current role, or mode, of the market. From this, you can adjust your trading strategy accordingly. You should use a trend-following strategy when the market is in the trend mode and a strategy exploiting the rapid turning points when the market is in the cycle mode.

A SPECTRUM OF SUPPORT

The quality and resolution of the cycle measurement can be determined from the spectrum display. A simple spike in the

spectrum window indicates that only a single, well-defined dominant cycle is present. If the display is a mushy bell-shaped curve,
the cyclic energy is spread over a range of cycle periods. You
should be less inclined to trade on the basis of cycles if the spectrum indicates this poor resolution of a dominant cycle. The poor
resolution means that there is a low confidence that a single
useful cycle exists. The spectrum also indicates the existence of
several simultaneous cycles when they occur. The relative amplitudes and phasing of multiple cycles can make interpretations of
market action more difficult. Multiple cycles can add together in
a complicated way, like biorhythms, to make forecasting more
problematical.

The spectrum can be used to anticipate the onset of a trend
using the principle of proportionality. MESA considers a trend as
a segment of a very long cycle. The principle of proportionality

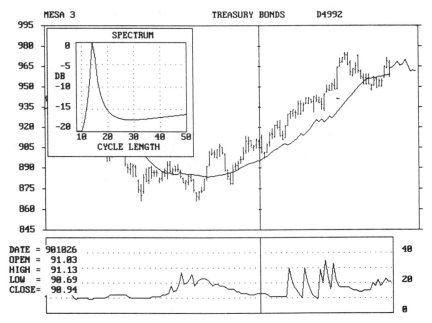

**Figure 11–2   Spectrum Display Lifts Off the Baseline Near the Beginning
of a Trend**

asserts that the longer cycles have a much larger amplitude than short-term cycles. MESA displays cycle periods up to 50 days on its spectrum display. Longer cycles are out of scale, so the display only catches a piece of the skirt of the bell-shaped spectrum. With reference to Figure 11–2, when the trend begins we only see the short-term cycle in the spectrum. Figure 11–3 shows the spectrum further into the trend. In this case, we start to see the skirt of the long-term cycle (trend) as the spectrum display lifts off the baseline near the right-hand side. Progressing in time, Figure 11–3 shows the development of the trend and the impact on the spectrum display. The spectrum is still further off the baseline, showing the trend is gaining strength. Finally, Figure 11–4 shows the trend well in force and the spectrum implying there is a very strong dominant cycle with a period much longer

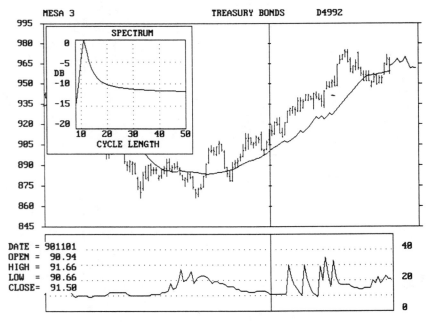

Figure 11–3 Further Lifting of the Spectrum from the Baseline Confirms Trend Development

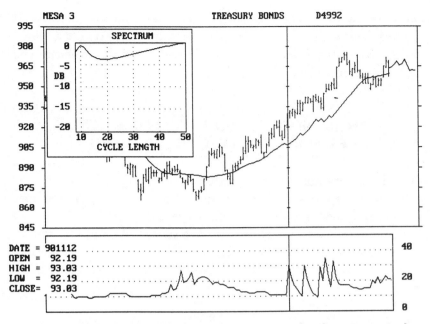

Figure 11-4   Skirt of the Trend Spectrum Swamps the Short-Term Cycle

than 50 days. The trend stays in force until the price next touches the instantaneous trendline.

A good spectrum does not necessarily imply that the prediction will be good. This is because the spectrum is formed from historical data while the prediction deals with the immediate future. For example, if the market has had several high-quality cycles, the spectrum will have high resolution. As we approach the cyclic peak, the prediction correctly predicts the expected downturn. But if an uptrend really has started, the prediction is dead wrong. The predicted direction for the next several days continues to be a downturn while the spectrum is still looking good and the uptrend is roaring off. Finally, the inertia of the historical data is overcome, and the predicted direction snaps to follow the trend. This snap often comes too late, on the order of three days after the trend has been declared, by using the failure-to-cross-the-trendline method. It is good practice to abandon trading using cyclic strategy immediately when the price fails to touch the trendline over the last half dominant cycle.

"IT IS DIFFICULT TO MAKE FORECASTS, ESPECIALLY ABOUT THE FUTURE"[1]

The MESA prediction has the greatest validity when the market is in the cycle mode and the measured dominant cycle has been stable for at least a half cycle. The expectation is that this stable dominant cycle will continue into the future. The prediction reflects this expectation, and additionally factors in the contribution of all the other measured cyclic components. The MESA

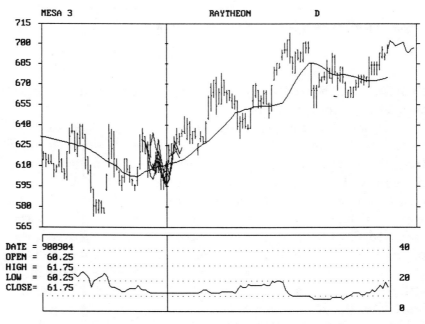

Figure 11–5 Successive Correlated Predictions Indicate a Cyclic Turning Point on 9/4/90

prediction is more successful predicting the timing of turning points rather than the level at which the turning points occur. The accuracy of the prediction can be enhanced by backtesting the prediction over the previous 3 to 5 days. Greater credibility can be given to predictions if they all reflect the same timing of the turning point. For example, Figure 11–5 shows the back-tested predictions for the 9 days preceding 9/4/90. Note the measured cycle was relatively stable during this period, and all the predictions consistently indicated the turning point with precision.

ADAPT AND SURVIVE!

Don't be a dinosaur with your trading strategy. The most important overall aspect of all these rules and tips is that you adapt to the market and take what the market gives you. Be flexible. Trade the trend mode using trend-following techniques when you have identified this mode is in force. You should be able to switch strategy back to cycle mode trading with equal facility. Chapter 12 provides an example of how this switching is done.

12

TRADING WITH MESA

The theoretical concepts previously discussed are applied to actual trading in this chapter. The S&P 500 perpetual contract for the 6 months preceding the October 1989 plunge was selected for this example because it has two trending periods interlaced with cyclic modes. A perpetual contract is used for illustration to obtain a single contiguous example with representative daily ranges over the entire time span. Actual contracts are often thinly traded early in their existence, and the chosen span would have necessarily included such cases if an actual contract were used. The MESA picture for this period is shown in Figure 12–1.

Figure 12–1 is representative of a typical MESA display. The daily price bars are plotted in the conventional manner, running from the low of the day to the high of the day. A tick on the left of the bar denotes the opening price and the tick on the right of the bar indicates the closing price for that day. The instantaneous trendline is overlaid on the price history so you can relate the price action to this trendline. We will discuss this relationship at length. The measured dominant cycle length is shown

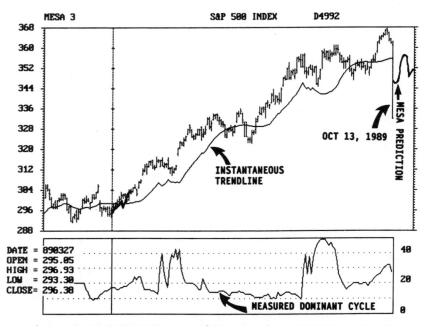

Figure 12-1   S&P 500 Perpetual Contract from 890207 to 891013

below the bar chart in the box scaled from zero to 50 days. In this box, the dominant cycle is plotted as a dot, and the dots are connected to form the cycle history display. MESA always makes a prediction from the last day in the file. In this case, the last day was 10/13/90, the day of the drop. This date is shown in the YYMMDD format in the tabular data in Figure 12-1, and the YYMMDD format will be used for date reference for the remainder of this chapter. The solid line from the middle of the last price bar is the prediction for the next 10 days. MESA predicted the recovery from this day with a high degree of accuracy although the large price movement invalidates cyclic analysis. The prediction uses the previous 30 days of data, and is based on total of that data rather than on the price of the last day.

CHAPTER 11 ISN'T ALWAYS BAD

The procedures of the previous chapter are used every day. The following is the daily routine in trading with MESA.

1. Measure the cyclic content. The dominant cycle and instantaneous trendline are automatically displayed.

2. Determine if the market is in the trend mode or the cycle mode by counting the daily bars backward from the current day, using half the number of the current measured dominant cycle. If the price has not touched the instantaneous trendline over this half-cycle period the market is in a trend mode. Otherwise, the market is in a cycle mode.

3. If the market is in a trend mode, ignore the predictions and the spectrum display. Use a trend-following strategy such as a double moving average or parabolic SAR (Stop And Reverse) to establish your trades and exits. Ignore cyclic analysis until the market again enters into the cycle mode.

4. If the market is in a cycle mode, first note if the cycle has been stable over the most recent half-cycle period. Be wary of any predictions if this stability does not exist. If the cycle has been stable, examine the prediction for an upcoming turning point so you can get prepared for your trade. Backtest the prediction for the previous 3 to 5 days to improve the validity of the prediction. Finally, examine the spectrum to ensure that a high-resolution cycle exists and to watch for the "tail" lifting off the baseline, foretelling the onset of a trend.

AULD LANG *SINE*

The trading example starts with the S&P 500 in the cycle mode. Each of the charts describing the analysis are captured from MESA screen displays. When the cursor is positioned to a point on the bar chart, the date and price display in the lower left-hand corner reflect the data for the position of the cursor. In Figure 12–2 the cursor is moved to 890327. Note that Figure 12–2 is basically the same as Figure 12–1 with different notation. For example, the predicted recovery on 891013 has not changed. Figure 12–2 shows that there was good cyclic activity in February and March (to the left of the cursor position) because the price was alternating back and forth across the instantaneous trendline. The measured cycle was as low as 10 days during this period. You can see these cycles in the price action. Starting at the leftmost edge of the screen, three successive highest highs and the two interstitial lowest lows are about 10 days apart. However, the 10-day cycle fails to continue after the third highest high. The result is that the spacing from the most recent lowest low had increased.

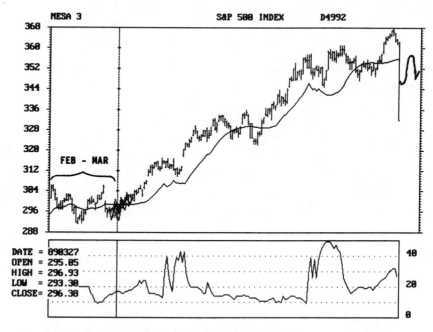

Figure 12–2 Good Cyclic Activity During February and March

Our analysis starts on 890327, a date that subsequently turned out to be the real onset of the trend. Following our daily procedure, we find that the backtested predictions all correlated, showing a move to the upside. The 18-day measured cycle also makes us feel good about going long because the cycle length correlates well with the last lowest low. Further, Figure 12–3 shows that the sharp, well-defined 18-day cycle has virtually all the energy in the short-term frequency domain. The single prediction for 890327 is also indicated.

Based on this analysis we enter the trade on the long side on 890327, as indicated by note (1) on the figure. We continue our daily routine, expecting to stay in the trade for 9 days because this is half the current dominant cycle.

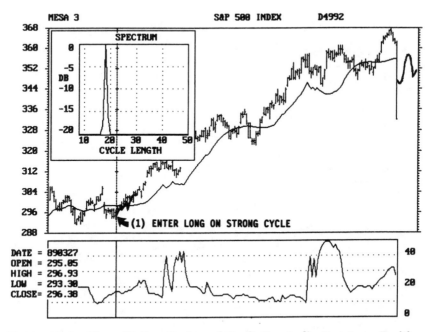

Figure 12–3   Clear 18-Day Cycle and Prediction Indicate a Long Position with High Confidence

THE TREND IS YOUR FRIEND

Allowing time to progress to 890413 as shown in Figure 12–4, we see the current measured cycle is 20 days, as shown in the spectrum display. The 3-day average of the cycle length displayed below the bar chart is 22 days. Note that the price has not touched the trendline in the last half cycle (10 days), so we declare an uptrend to be in force, as indicated by note (3). If we had been really lucky (by being inattentive to MESA signals, for example) we would still have had our long position from the entry on 890327 (see Figures 12–2 and 12–3). A more likely situation is that we would have gone short 4 or 5 days before 890413 on the basis of a MESA prediction, predicting a cyclic downturn at the point marked by note (2). In fact, you can see this downturn starting to form 5 days to the left of the cursor. The cycle mode

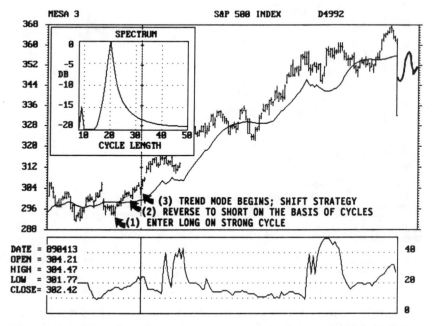

Figure 12–4 Trend Mode Begins When Price Fails to Cross the Trendline for a Half Cycle

failed. If we had gone short on the basis of cyclic predictions, the only tactic to employ on 890413 is to exit that short for a loss as quickly as possible. Then we would shift strategy to trade the S&P 500 in the trend mode. In the trend mode, one tactic you can employ is to use the instantaneous trendline as the value of your stop on a day-by-day basis. Setting your stop this way has the disadvantage that the gap between the price and your stop can sometimes be large, exceeding the daily limit move. This gap is not terribly significant if you have established a profit position because it is your intent to hold the position until the trend mode is over. Nonetheless, more conventional trend-following techniques, such as a parabolic SAR, are recommended when the market is in a trend mode.

Figure 12–5 shows that the trend mode ends on 890615 when the price again touches the trendline at the location of note (4). A trend-following system with a relatively tight stop

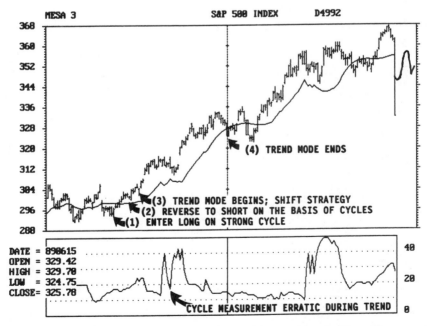

Figure 12–5 Trend Mode Ends When Price Touches the Trendline

probably would have had us exit the long trade before MESA declares the trend to be at an end. Note that the dominant cycle measurement has spikes, indicative of an erratic measurement, while the trend mode is in force. This erratic cyclic behavior when the market is in the trend mode is the reason we ignore all cyclic outputs, such as the prediction. The dominant cycle measurements calm down and again become consistent near the end of the trend mode. Since the dominant cycle measurement has more stability near the end of the trend mode, we can have greater confidence in the MESA predictions.

"IT'S DEJA VU ALL OVER AGAIN"[1]

We arrived at the cycle mode again, and so we initiate our daily procedures again. Following the daily procedure, we tested

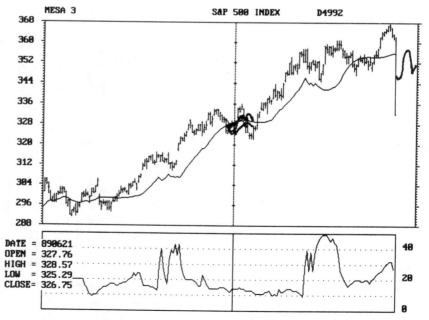

Figure 12–6 Predictions Are Consistent in New Cycle Mode

successive predictions for consistency after again entering the cycle mode as shown in Figure 12–6. We also note that the cycle measurement has been stable for almost one full cycle length. We supplement our analysis with the spectrum display shown in Figure 12–7. The 16-day cycle is of relatively high resolution. Based on these factors, we would enter into a long trade when MESA gave a prediction for a cyclic low on 890621, depicted by note (5). We had an open position between the end of the trend and the new long entry made on the basis of cycles.

Continuing in the cycle mode, we use the predictions to anticipate a turning point on 890626, a half cycle into the future. Figure 12–8 shows that the backtested predictions correlate, making us feel warm about reversing to a short position. Further, the spectrum shows that only a single high-resolution 14-day

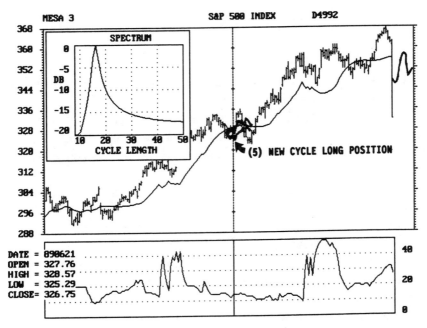

Figure 12–7 Good Spectrum Display Confirms Cycle Mode

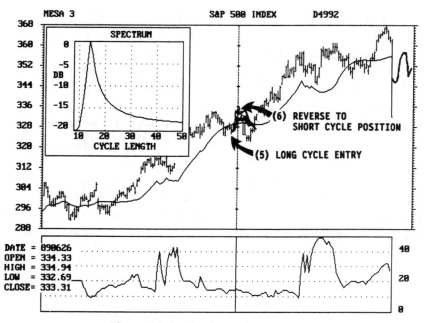

Figure 12–8   Cycle Mode Continues

cycle exists at the current time. Using all these signals, we go short on 890626 as indicated by note (6).

Still continuing in the cycle mode, a turning point to the upside is anticipated for 890705 on the basis of MESA predictions. Figure 12–9 shows the backtested predictions correlate to improve the probability that the prediction is a good one, with the entry depicted at note (7). The spectrum shows that measured cycle still has high resolution and the cycle length has been reduced slightly to 12 days. We now reverse to the long side based on this analysis.

Also note that the predictions in Figure 12–9 indicate a cyclic turning point about 6 days into the future. At this point we anticipate staying in the long position for about 6 days, half the current, measured dominant cycle length.

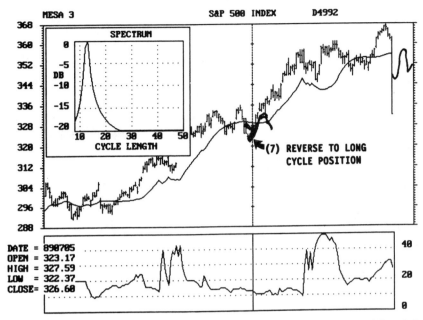

Figure 12–9 **Correlated Predictions Indicate a Long Entry with High Confidence**

THE FRIEND RETURNS

Figure 12–10 displays the cursor at 890717, 8 days after the cursor position of Figure 12–9. The cycle measurement remains stable. MESA had predicted a downturn 3 days prior to this point, and we would be in a short position on the basis of the predicted cyclic turning point, as indicated at note (8). However, the price has not touched the trendline in the past 5 days. Five days is half the measured dominant cycle at this time. Therefore, an uptrend is again declared to be in force. Being in a short position due to cycles, we should exit this position immediately and switch strategy back to trend mode strategy. We should now be on the long side of the trade entering into the trend mode, as depicted by note (9). Careful examination of Figure 12–10 shows that the

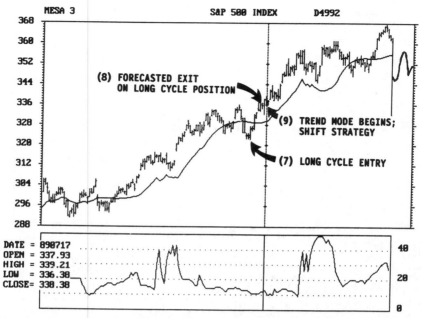

Figure 12–10 New Trend Mode Begins When Price Fails to Cross the Trendline

cycle mode attempted the downturn about 3 days to the left of the cursor, but the cycle mode had failed. These failures are extremely hard to see in real time, and only become apparent after the trend mode has been identified.

Figure 12–11 shows the spectrum measurement taken only 2 days after we declared the trend to be in force. The resolution of the measured cycles is dreadful. This poor resolution adds vigor to our conviction that the market is in a trend mode. The dominant cycle below the bar chart appears to be stable even entering into the trend mode, but the resolution during this period is poor. The poor cycle resolution continues to give strength to our selection of the trend strategy.

Figure 12–12 shows the second trend mode continues until 890913, when the price again touches the trendline. Measurement of the dominant cycle is erratic during this trend mode period.

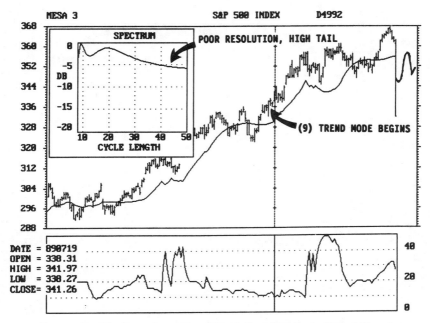

Figure 12–11   Poor Spectrum Resolution Confirms Trend Onset

The cycle mode then is in effect from the cursor position to the end of the chart. We would have no position for a short while after the end of the trend mode but then would establish a long position because the measured 20-day dominant cycle is consistent with being one full cycle length from the previous lowest low.

YES, MESA PREDICTED THE PLUNGE

Almost every trading system has claimed to have anticipated the October 1989 market drop, with perfect hindsight. MESA showed the market was in a cycle mode during October 1989. Using consistent rules for the cycle mode, MESA would establish a short position prior to the drop without requiring hindsight. Four correlated predictions prior to 891012 showed the high point

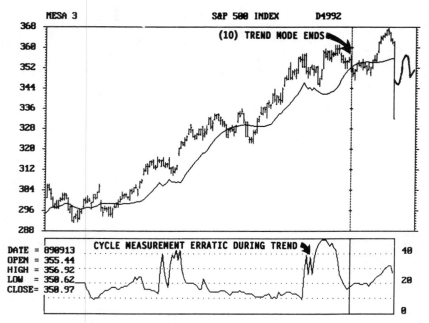

Figure 12–12   Trend Mode Ends When Price Touches the Trendline

of the market was projected to occur on that date, as shown in Figure 12–13. The measured 30-day cycle correlates well with the occurrence of the previous highest high, and 891012 is 15 days (a half dominant cycle length) from our previous long position. The shift of the measured dominant cycle from 20 days is consistent with the correlation of the lowest lows just as the market entered the cycle mode. Having followed the MESA analysis, you can now see that this prediction was not produced magically.

Application of science, not magic, leads to profit in trading. MESA is the logical application of the science of cycles that allows you to differentiate between the cycle mode and trend mode. While in the cycle mode, MESA allows you to anticipate the turning points through the predictions formed by allowing its digital filter to ring out into the future. Note that throughout the entire discussion of the trading example if we covered the

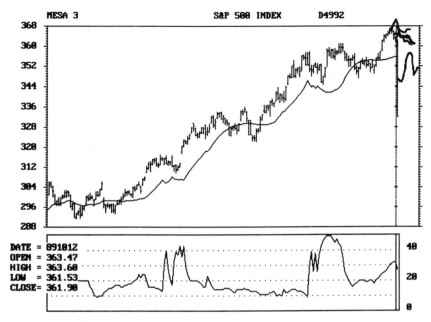

Figure 12–13 Four Correlated Predictions Establish a Cyclic Short Position Before the Plunge

future activity to blind ourselves to the upcoming events, the analysis would be unchanged. The analysis sometimes leads to error. The cycle mode strategies don't work when the cycle fades. However, the procedures that have been outlined allow you to adjust quickly to the changing market conditions.

Cycles work for me. They can work for you too! Good Trading!

GLOSSARY

ALIASING False reconstruction of a signal resulting from sampling at a rate below the Nyquist sampling criterion. Stagecoach wheels appearing to turn backward in a movie is an example of aliasing.

AMPLITUDE The size of the cycle swing. Usually expressed as half the difference between the peak value and minimum value of the cycle function. Amplitude is the length of the cycle phasor.

AUTOCORRELATION A function measuring the correlation of a wave shape in the time domain with itself shifted over a range of lag periods. For example, a sine wave is perfectly correlated with itself when shifted by exactly one cycle.

BEL The logarithm of a power ratio. Named after Alexander Graham Bell for his work in audio research.

BROWNIAN MOTION Random three-dimensional motion. Can be visualized as the path of a molecule of air in a vacuum jar in the absence of electrostatic or gravitational influences.

CONVERGENCE Situation when the rate of change of price is the same as the rate of change of an indicator, for example, when both price and momentum are increasing.

CONVOLUTION A method of computing the output of a filter in the time domain using the time domain input waveform and the time-folded impulse response of the filter.

CYCLE   A motion where the element returns to the point of origin after a period of time.

DECI-   A prefix meaning one tenth.

DECIBEL   One tenth the logarithm of a power ratio.

DECIMATION   Literally means taking every tenth, but in practice it usually means taking every second one of a set. Experimenters sometimes take a long history of closely spaced samples to obtain the high-frequency components by analysis without aliasing. Samples can be removed to compute the lower frequency components to reduce computation time.

DETRENDED SYNTHETIC PRICE   A function that is in phase with the dominant cycle of real price data. It is computed by subtracting the half-dominant-cycle SMA from the quarter-dominant-cycle SMA (or equivalent EMAs).

DIFFUSION EQUATION   A differential equation describing the way heat travels up a spoon when placed in a hot cup of coffee or the path of particles in a smoke plume leaving a smokestack. By analogy, it can describe market action under conditions satisfying the drunkard's walk.

DIVERGENCE   When the rate of change of price is opposite the rate of change of an indicator. For example, price is increasing and momentum is decreasing.

EHLERS LEADING INDICATOR   An indicator giving an advance indication of a cyclic turning point. It is computed by subtracting the quarter-dominant-cycle SMA (or EMA equivalent) from the detrended synthetic price. BUY and SELL signals arise when this indicator crosses the detrended synthetic price.

ELI   Acronym for Ehlers Leading Indicator.

EMA   Acronym for exponential moving average.

ENTROPY   A measure of unavailable energy, or disorder. Used both in thermodynamics and information theory. Coined from the Greek language to mean "transformation."

EXPONENTIAL MOVING AVERAGE   A recursive calculation for a moving average accomplished by adding a fraction times current data to the product of the complement of that fraction and the previous exponential moving average value. Sometimes called an infinite impulse response (IIR) filter. The time response to an impulse input is an exponential decay of amplitude.

FAST FOURIER TRANSFORM   A method for calculating Fourier coefficients by reducing the calculations to the order of N*log(N), where N is the sample length.

FIRST-ORDER   A term meaning a simple approximation. The term is derived from using only the first term of an Nth-order power series expansion of a function as an approximation.

FOURIER SERIES   The theory that any arbitrary waveform can be synthesized, or described, by an infinite series of sines and cosines. Each term in the series can have an independent amplitude and phase.

FOURIER TRANSFORM   A symmetrical process to describe a function in the frequency domain, given its time domain response or to describe the function in the time domain, given its frequency domain response.

FREQUENCY   The rate at which cycles occur. For example, 2000 revolutions per minute is a frequency.

IMPULSE   A mathematical function that exists only at the origin. The impulse has an infinite height and zero width, such that the area within the impulse is unity.

JERK   The derivative, or rate of change of an impulse. Can be visualized as comprising a positive impulse and a negative impulse.

KINETIC ENERGY   The energy attributed to a mass due to its motion.

LOW PASS FILTER   A filter that allows only low-frequency components of a signal to pass to the output, blocking high-frequency components. Often used as a smoothing filter.

MAXIMUM ENTROPY   A formalism describing optimal calculation procedures. For example, if all the information is extracted from a signal, the residual is left with maximum entropy. The residual can be tested for information content to see if, in fact, it has maximum entropy.

MAXIMUM ENTROPY SPECTRAL ANALYSIS   A method of spectral estimation generated by Dr. John Parker Burg.

MESA   The name of a cycles-based trading program, and the company producing this program. MESA is an acronym for maximum entropy spectral analysis.

MOMENTUM (MECHANICAL)   The property of a moving body that determines the amount of time to bring it to rest under the action of a constant force. In the market, it usually means taking the difference between prices at a fixed interval.

NOISE   All functions that do not contain information. Static hiss from a radio is an example of noise. The only information this hiss contains is that the radio is turned on.

NYQUIST SAMPLING LIMITATION   Any band-limited function can be faithfully reproduced from samples taken at least twice per cycle.

PERIOD   The length of a cycle. Period is the reciprocal of frequency.

PHASE   The relative position within a cycle. Phase is usually expressed as an angle referenced to the origin. There are 360 degrees of phase in a cycle.

PHASOR   A rotating vector depicting the relative phase in a cycle.

PI   The ratio of the circumference to the radius of a circle, 3.1415926. . .

POWER SPECTRAL DENSITY   A continuous function describing the power function in the frequency domain. It is the discrete-time Fourier transform of the autocorrelation sequence of a sampled function.

PREWHITENING   Removing known frequency components prior to analysis.

PRIMITIVE   A primary function, not derived. Used here, sine waves are primitives from which complex waveforms can be synthesized. See Fourier series.

RAMP   A function having a constant slope beginning at the origin.

RANDOM VARIABLE   A variable that can take on values at random from a continuum of possible values.

RELATIVE STRENGTH INDEX   A normalized trading indicator formed by the ratio of the sum of the closes up to the sum of the closes up plus the sum of the closes down over a selected period of time.

RESONANCE   A condition where oscillation is allowed at one frequency only.

RSI   The acronym for relative strength index.

SEASONAL   A pattern that repeats over any 12-month period.

SIMPLE MOVING AVERAGE   A simple average of N samples is the sum of the samples, each weighted by N. This average becomes a moving average by simultaneously adding a new weighted sample and dropping off the oldest weighted sample.

SIN(X)/X   A mathematical function where X is expressed in radians. This is the Fourier transform of a pulse with uniform amplitude.

SLOPE   A rate of change.

SMA   Acronym for simple moving average.

SMOOTHING   The process of removing high-frequency variations by low pass filtering. Smoothing is always accompanied by time delay.

STEP FUNCTION   A function having an abrupt discontinuity at the origin and uniform amplitude everywhere else.

STOCHASTIC INDICATOR   A normalized indicator where the difference between the recent highest high and the current closing price is divided by the difference between the recent highest high and the recent lowest low. "Recent" is a time space chosen by the technical analyst.

STOCHASTIC VARIABLE   The outcome in an experiment having an exhaustive set of mutually exclusive events and a set of probabilities of occurrences, so-called because taking any one of the possible values is a matter of chance.

SYNTHETIC PRICE   A function that is in phase with the dominant cycle of real price data. It is computed by subtracting the half-dominant-cycle SMA from the quarter-dominant-cycle SMA (or equivalent EMAs).

TAPERING   A weighting multiplier used to shape the data within a sample window. Tapering is used to reduce the sidelobe responses such as in the sin (X)/X function that result from the Fourier transform of a rectangular window.

TELEGRAPHER'S EQUATION   A differential equation that describes the waves traveling on a pair of telegraph wires. By analogy, it describes the market when the market is in the cycle mode.

TREND   A general linear rate of change. In the market, trends are often identified by drawing lines between successive highest highs or successive lowest lows.

WINDOWING   Taking a sample of data representative of the longer data stream. Mathematically, this is equivalent to multiplying the data by one within the window length and multiplying by zero outside the window. Rectangular windowing results in a sin (X)/X Fourier transform response being superimposed on the Fourier transform of the real signal.

ENDNOTES

CHAPTER 1

1. J. D. Hurst, *The Profit Magic of Stock Transaction Timing* (Prentice-Hall, 1970). p. 31.

2. G. I. Taylow, "Diffusion by Continuous Movements," *Proc. London Math. Soc.* 20 (1920): 197–212. Proceedings of the London Mathematical Society.

3. G. H. Weiss and R. J. Rubin, "Random Walks: Theory and Selected Applications," Advances in *Chemical Physics,* Volume 52 John Wiley & Sons, 1983.

CHAPTER 3

1. J. M. Hurst, The Profit Magic of Stock Transaction Timing (Prentice-Hall, 1970). p. 51–67.

CHAPTER 4

1. J. Ehlers, "Moving Averages and Smoothing Filters," *Technical Analysis of Stocks and Commodities* (March 1989): p. 42.

2. J. K. Hutson, "Moving Averages versus Exponential Moving Averages," *Technical Analysis of Stocks and Commodities* (May/June 1984). p. 107.

CHAPTER 6

1. J. Welles Wilder, Jr., "New Concepts in Technical Trading Systems," *Trend Research* (1978), Section VI.

2. Gerald Appel, *The Major Trend Power Index.* Copyright by Scientific Investment Systems, Inc., 62 Wellesley Street West, Toronto, Canada.

3. Y. W. Lee, Statistical Theory of Communication (John Wiley & Sons, 1960), Chapter 15.

CHAPTER 8

1. Stan Ehrlich, Ehrlich Commodity Futures, 1683 Novato Blvd. Suite 2A, Novato, CA 94947.

2. J. P. Burg, *Maximum Entropy Spectral Analysis* (Paper presented at the 37th Annual Meeting, Society of Exploration Geophysicists, Oklahoma City, OK, 31 October 1967).

3. J. P. Burg, *Maximum Entropy Spectral Analysis* (Doctoral dissertation, electrical engineering, Stanford University, Stanford, CA, 1975).

CHAPTER 9

1. W. G. Hood, "Polynomial Curve Fitter," *BYTE* (June 1987): 155.

2. A. Van Den Bos, "Alternative Interpretation of Maximum Entropy Spectrum Analysis," *IEEE Transactions Information Theory* (1971): IT-17, 493. 1971.

3. R. L. Miller, "A New Cycle Analysis Trading Technique," *Technical Analysis of Stocks & Commodities* (May 1989): 22.

CHAPTER 11

1. Attributed to Samuel Goldwyn.

CHAPTER 12

1. Attributed to Yogi Berra.

INDEX